Table of C

Introduction ....
   Why Do You Need This Book? 1
   How to Use This Book 2
   Don't Miss Our Web Site 2

Chapter 1: Getting Acquainted with FrontPage 2000 5
   Installing and Running FrontPage 2000 6
   Using FrontPage's Main Screen 8
      The Big Picture 8
      Page view 9
      Folders view 11
      Reports view 11
      Navigation view 13
      Hyperlinks view 14
      Tasks view 14
   Getting Help 15

Chapter 2: Creating Your First Web Site 17
   Planning Your Web Site 18
      Choose your subject 18
      Define your goals 19
      Target your audience 20
      Storyboard your site 21
      Find a Web server 22
   Creating Your First Web Site 23
   Working with Your New Web 26
      Closing and opening your Web 26
      Opening your home page 27
      Saving your work 28
      Closing your home page 28
      Deleting an unwanted Web 29

Chapter 3: Working with Your Web Pages 30
   Opening Your Web Pages 30
   Adding Text to Your Home Page 31
      Entering and editing text 31
      Cutting, copying, and pasting text 32
      Aligning text to the left, right, or center 32
      Indenting text 33

Formatting Your Text 34
   Changing text font and size 34
   Making text underlined, bold, or italicized 35
   Choosing different colors for your text 36
Deleting Material 37
Previewing Your Work 37
   Previewing in FrontPage 37
   Previewing in your Web browser 38

Chapter 4: Customizing Your Web Site 40
Adding More Web Pages to Your Site 40
   Adding New Web Pages 41
   Making your new pages part of your Web 41
   Giving your new pages titles 43
Choosing a Theme for Your Web 44
Adding Shared Borders and
Navigation Buttons 46
   Naming your new Web pages 49
   Working with navigation bars 50
   Working with shared borders 52

Chapter 5: Beefing Up Your Web Pages with Links, Lists, and Pictures 54
Linking Web Pages 55
   Creating links to external sites 55
   Creating an e-mail link 57
Putting Your Information into Lists 59
   Creating bulleted lists 59
   Creating numbered lists 60
Adding Clip Art and Pictures to Your Page 60
   Using clip art in your Web page 61
   Adding pictures to your Web page 63

Chapter 6: Creating Tables 66
Creating a Table 67
Working with Table Content 70
   Adding material to a table 70
   Aligning items in your table cells 71
Working with the Table Itself 72
   Changing the width of your table 73
   Aligning your table on your Web page 74

Adding and removing rows and columns 74
Working with borders 75

Chapter 7: Adding Extras: Multimedia, Dynamic HTML, and More 77
Setting a Target Web Browser 78
Adding Sounds and Video 80
    Adding background sound 80
    Adding inline sound 83
    Adding video 84
Adding Dynamic HTML to Your Pages 85
Adding More Extras 86
    Using hover buttons 86
    Adding a marquee 87
    Inserting Symbols 88
    Adding horizontal lines 88

Chapter 8: Publishing Your Web Site on the Internet 90
Getting Things Ready 91
    Preparing your computer 91
    Your Web site 92
Finding a Server 93
    Using your Internet Service Provider's server 93
    Finding a Registered Web Presence Provider 94
    Determining Your Web Address 95
Publishing Your Web Site 96

Chapter 9: Maintaining and Updating Your Web Site 99
Maintaining Your Web Site 99
    Spell-checking individual Web pages 100
    Spell checking your site 101
    Using the Site Summary report 102
    Working with hyperlinks 103
    Viewing files that aren't linked 105
Updating Your Web Site 107

CliffsNotes Review 109
Q&A 109
Scenarios 110
Visual Test 111
Consider This 112
Practice Project 112

CliffsNotes Resource Center **113**
   Books 113
   Internet 114
   Magazines & Other Media 115
   Send Us Your Favorite Tips 116

Index **117**

INTRODUCTION

We live in exciting times. The Internet has revolutionized communication, and the World Wide Web reaches into millions of homes and businesses 24 hours a day, 7 days a week. Creating a Web site gives you unparalleled power to express your ideas. Think about that for a minute. Everyone connected to the Internet with access to a Web browser — your family, friends, associates, customers, and so forth — all over the globe can visit your Web site and benefit from your thoughts on *any subject you choose.*

Microsoft FrontPage 2000 is a tool you can use to make this all happen. FrontPage enables you to build wonderfully creative Web sites filled with your own Web pages. FrontPage also makes creating your own Web sites about as easy as creating a document in a word processing program. CliffNotes *Creating Your First Web Site with FrontPage 2000* introduces you to FrontPage and shows you how you can use this powerful program to create, publish, and maintain your very own Web site.

Why Do You Need This Book?

Can you answer yes to any of these questions?

- Need to learn about Microsoft FrontPage 2000 fast?
- Don't have time to read 500 pages on FrontPage or Web publishing?
- Want to publish your very own Web site and be able to add interesting pages to it?

If so, then CliffsNotes *Creating Your First Web Site with FrontPage 2000* is for you!

How to Use This Book

You can read this book straight through or just look for the information you need. You can find information on a particular topic in a number of ways: You can locate your topic in the Table of Contents, read the In This Chapter list at the beginning of each chapter, or search the index in the back of the book. To reinforce your learning, check out the Resource Center or test your knowledge in the Review section. To help you find important information in the book, look for the following icons in the text:

If you see a Remember icon, make a mental note of this text — it's worth keeping in mind.

If you see a Tip icon, you'll know that you've run across a helpful hint, uncovered a secret, or received good advice.

The Warning icon alerts you to something that could be dangerous, requires special caution, or should be avoided.

Don't Miss Our Web Site

Keep up with the exciting world of FrontPage 2000 and the World Wide Web by visiting the CliffsNotes Web site at www.cliffsnotes.com. Here's what you find:

- Interactive tools that are fun and informative.
- Links to interesting Web sites.
- Additional resources to help you continue your learning.

At www.cliffsnotes.com, you can even register for a new feature called CliffsNotes Daily, which offers you newsletters on a variety of topics, delivered right to your e-mail inbox each business day.

If you haven't yet discovered the Internet and are wondering how to get online, pick up CliffsNotes *Getting On the Internet*, new from CliffsNotes. You'll learn just what you need to make your online connection quickly and easily. See you at www.cliffsnotes.com!

CHAPTER 1
GETTING ACQUAINTED WITH FRONTPAGE 2000

IN THIS CHAPTER

- Exploring what you can do with FrontPage
- Installing and running Front Page
- Acquainting yourself with the FrontPage main screen
- Getting help from FrontPage

If you've seen the popularity of the Internet and Web sites explode dramatically over the last few years and want to join the excitement, Microsoft FrontPage 2000 is the software program for you. Microsoft FrontPage 2000 (which I call FrontPage throughout this book) allows you to create and maintain Web sites that share your take on Life, Liberty, and the Pursuit of Happiness with the world at large. Having a Web site is like having your own private printing press without all that messy ink on your fingers. Just think: You can use FrontPage to quickly, cheaply, but professionally publish your thoughts to a potentially immense audience.

In case you're new to the World Wide Web and the world of Web publishing, a Web *site* (also called a Web or just a site) is simply a collection of Web *pages* that you connect via *hyperlinks* to form a cohesive presentation of ideas and information. You can find Web sites online as part of the World Wide Web, a very popular component of the Internet. Web pages are documents that may contain text, pictures, animation, video or other items and are viewed with a Web *browser* (a special bit of software), such as Microsoft Internet Explorer or Netscape Navigator.

In this chapter, I introduce you to FrontPage and show you how to find your way around the program. I also show you how you can use FrontPage in every phase of your site's development, from building your site and creating the Web pages that form the site to publishing your site on the Internet and keeping it in working order.

Installing and Running FrontPage 2000

The first task you should accomplish is to install FrontPage 2000 to your hard drive. You may have purchased FrontPage as a stand-alone, boxed software product or as part of Microsoft Office 2000 Premier Edition. Either way, installing FrontPage is straightforward. After you put the program's Installation CD in your computer's CD-ROM drive, the Setup program walks you through every step of the process.

When you install FrontPage 2000, you can choose between a Typical or Custom installation. Choosing Typical is the most straightforward, but Custom allows you to choose several additional components. Table 1-1 shows all the additional parts of FrontPage that you can install. If you choose Custom, I recommend that you install the tutorial, help, and additional themes at a minimum. The other components aren't necessary for you to begin using FrontPage.

Table 1-1: FrontPage Components

If You Want...	Install This Component...
Assistance learning FrontPage	Tutorial (recommended)
Access to FrontPage help	Help (recommended)
Advanced examples	Samples
To use FrontPage Server Extensions	Server Extensions Resource Kit
To remotely administer your Server Extensions	Server Extensions Admin Forms
More themes than you can shake a stick at	Additional Themes (recommended)

If you are upgrading from FrontPage 98 or other earlier version, you should first uninstall that version of FrontPage. To uninstall an old version of FrontPage, choose Start⇨Settings⇨Control Panel to open your Control Panel folder. Then, select Add/Remove Programs. Doing so opens the Add/Remove Programs Properties dialog box. Find your old version of FrontPage, select it, and then click the Add/Remove button. When FrontPage is finished uninstalling, click OK to close the Add/Remove Programs Properties dialog box.

You can start FrontPage just like the other programs you have installed on your computer. Follow these steps to run FrontPage:

1. Click the Start button.

2. Choose Programs⇨Microsoft FrontPage.

When FrontPage launches, your screen should look just like Figure 1-1.

Nothing really fancy happens when you first run FrontPage; you just see a new, blank Web page in the right part of the screen, waiting for you to begin working. This behavior is very much like Microsoft Word, which opens a new, blank Word document every time you run it. Notice the vertical line in the blank document? This is called the *insertion point*, which blinks at you so that you can find it easily. When you begin typing, your text appears at the insertion point just as it does in Microsoft Word. Go ahead, try it to see what happens! I cover the main screen and all its different pieces in the next section.

Figure 1-1: Run FrontPage to begin your Web publishing career.

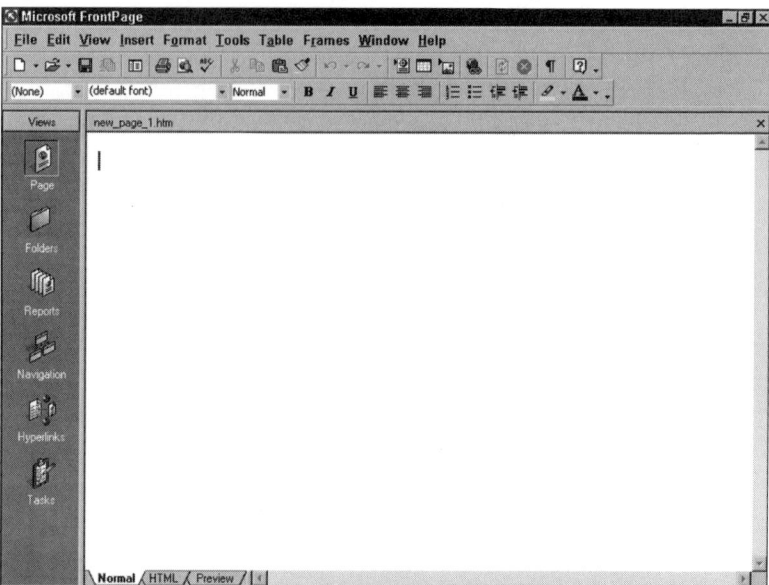

Using FrontPage's Main Screen

The folks who designed FrontPage went out of their way to set up the program so that you can create your entire Web site, complete with Web pages, with the help of one easy-to-use main screen. There you find all the tool and menu bars you'll ever need to create your Web site, edit the Web pages that make up your site, manage your Web's files and folders, publish, and maintain your site. Don't worry if you're not familiar with all these tasks yet. You can learn about some of them as you read more about the FrontPage screens and as you make your way through this book.

The Big Picture

Time to take a closer look at the FrontPage main screen. Along the top you see the Menu, Standard, and Formatting toolbars. The Menu toolbar, which gives you access to all

FrontPage features, works just like the menus in other Microsoft Office software programs. You can create new Webs, edit and save pages, insert objects into Web pages, and much more by using the different menus.

You should know that FrontPage 2000 uses "smart menus." These menus show you the most basic menu choices and "remember" the ones that you use often. If you don't see a menu item that I describe in this book, move your mouse over the double arrows at the bottom of a menu. This action expands the menu and shows you all the possible choices. The buttons on the Standard and Formatting toolbars provide a quick alternative to the menus. They contain many of the features you use most often, and you can access them just by clicking the button.

Along the left side of the screen is the Views bar, with six different icons. From top to bottom they are Page, Folders, Reports, Navigation, Hyperlinks, and Tasks. Each icon represents a different way to view your Web site. If you want to switch views, click a different icon in the Views bar. You can tell which view is active by looking for the icon that looks pressed in. The following sections explain each view.

I've created a small sample Web site to illustrate the FrontPage screens that I describe in the rest of this chapter. Although you may not understand yet how I've created this site, don't worry about that for now. You'll soon be able to create your own snazzy Web site that will probably surpass mine!

Page view

The topmost icon on the Views bar is the Page View icon. Figure 1-2 shows you a document's appearance in Page view. Notice that the Web page looks something like a document might appear in Word (although definitely more exciting). A snazzy Guitar Home Web page is a far cry from the boring form letters most people write on their computers. FrontPage makes such snazziness child's play by letting you add neat banners, boxes, borders, pictures, and of course, text with a few clicks of the mouse and a few keyboard commands.

Figure 1-2:   Use FrontPage's Page view to edit your Web pages.

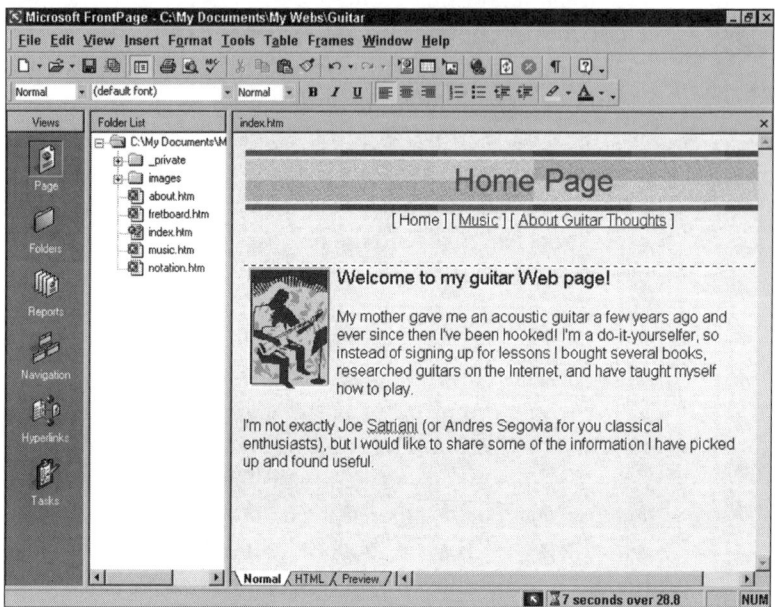

The menu, toolbars, and Views bar stay the same in each view. In the Page, Folders, Navigation, and Hyperlinks views, however, you see a Folder list beside the Views bar. The Folder list conveniently shows all the files and folders that belong to your Web site. The Folder list works similarly to a normal Windows Explorer window. You can drag and drop files, rename them, and even delete files and folders.

If you don't see the Folder list, select View➪Folder list.

You actually work on your Web pages in the main part of the Page view window. This window works just like the main screen in Microsoft Word. Just start typing to enter text!

Notice the three tabs down at the bottom of the main screen? You'll mostly use just two of these: Normal and Preview. The Normal tab puts you in Edit mode; the Preview tab displays your Web page the way it will appear to a visitor viewing it in his or her Web browser. (Be forewarned. You can't edit your pages in Preview.)

Clicking the HTML tab uncovers all the nasty-looking programming code (called *HyperText Markup Language*) that Web pages need to display correctly on the Web. The beauty of FrontPage is that it lets you keep all that nasty code in the background if you don't want to see it. Keep things simple: Leave the HTML tab alone until you have a lot of experience under your belt.

Folders view

Going down the Views bar, the next icon you see is the Folders View icon. The Folders view displays the folder in which your Web site is stored on your hard drive. It also displays your Web site's files and useful information such as their size and who created them. Use this view to manage your files just as you do in Windows Explorer, performing chores such as

- Moving, copying, deleting, and renaming files
- Adding new Web pages to your site
- Creating new folders within your Web site

In Folders view, the filenames for all Web pages have an .htm extension. Other file types, such as pictures, have different extensions. For example, graphics have a .gif, .jpeg, or .png extension.

Reports view

Use the Reports view to gather important information about your Web site. When you select this view, you receive a Site

CliffsNotes Creating Your First Web Site with FrontPage 2000

Summary report, shown in Figure 1-3. This report shows you at a glance the most important information about your site. Look at each entry in the report. Unlinked Files, for example, tells you whether you have any Web pages that aren't connected to any other page in your site. Slow Pages informs you of any of your Web pages that will take a long time to download. Double-click an item to open the complete report for it. A complete report offers more details than are shown in the Site Summary report (it is, after all, a summary).

Figure 1-3: Get information about your Web site from the Reports view.

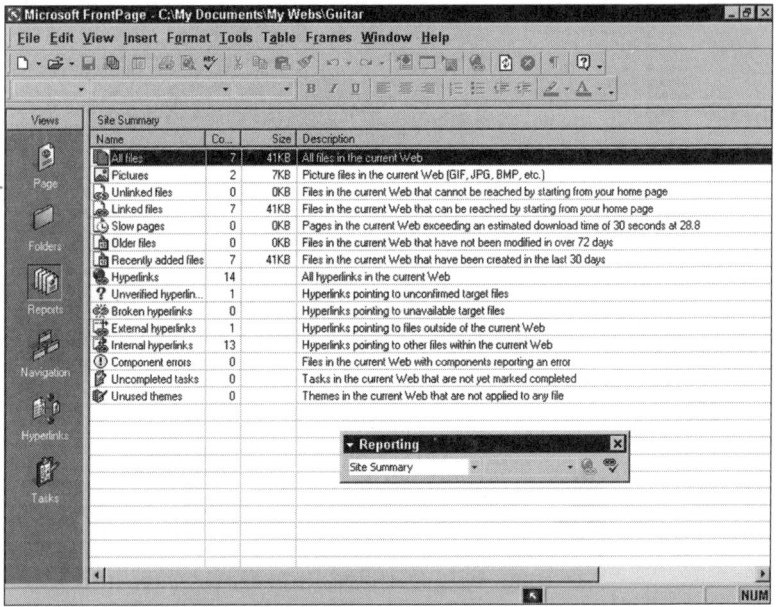

Notice the floating Reporting toolbar in the lower portion of Figure 1-3? FrontPage often uses these floating toolbars with drop-down menus to give you different ways of accomplishing the same tasks. In this book, I have tried to show you the easiest way to perform any task, but with these toolbars, you can decide which way is best for you. The Reporting toolbar allows you to select a report by clicking the down arrow beside Site Summary and choosing another report.

Navigation view

If you want to see an overview of how your Web site is set up and change it if you like, use the Navigation view. The Navigation view, shown in Figure 1-4, gives you a graphical representation of the relationships among all the pages in your site. Your *home page*, the first Web page visitors will see, is at the top of your site. The rest of your pages are linked beneath your home page, and people can visit them by clicking links from your home page.

Figure 1-4: Drag-and-drop Web pages to change the overall structure of your Web site in Navigation view.

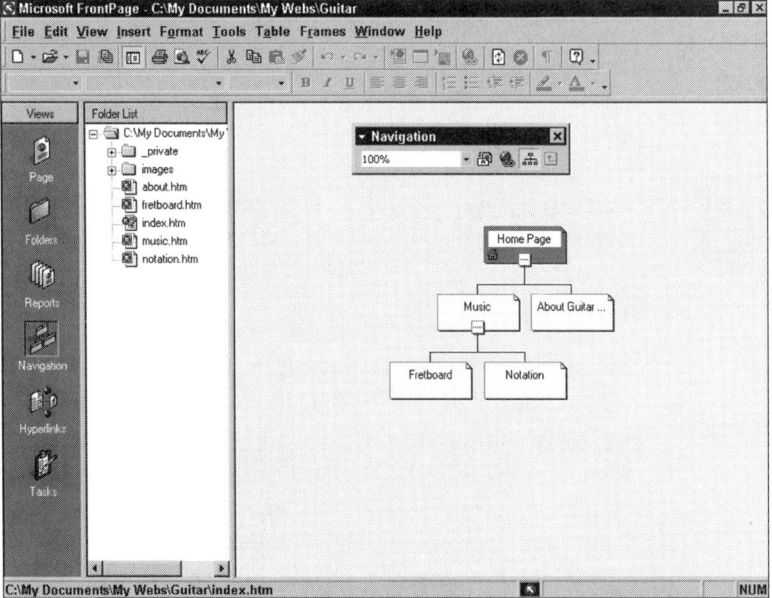

You can use the Navigation view to add pages to your Web site's structure, change the structure of your site (in other words, modify where each page fits in relation to your other pages), or just to keep an eye on the Big Picture. FrontPage uses this information behind the scenes to figure out how to connect your pages together if you decide to use navigation bars. (For more on navigation bars, see Chapter 4.)

Hyperlinks view

The Hyperlinks view shows all the hyperlinks, also called *links*, for a selected page within your Web site. Hyperlinks are the glue that holds your Web pages together to form a site. They also allow people to visit sites that are not part of your Web site. A hyperlink consists of a source and a destination. The source, which is generally displayed as underlined text, is the word, phrase, or picture that people click to take them to another Web page. The destination, which is not displayed on the Web page, is the Web address of the page to which you are linking.

Click an .htm file in the Folder List to select a Web page. An icon representing the Web page appears in the main window and the hyperlinks to and from the page are shown, as illustrated in Figure 1-5.

Hyperlinks connect your Web pages. Use the Hyperlinks view to track, maintain, and troubleshoot all your hyperlinks.

Tasks view

Choose the Tasks view to show all the tasks currently scheduled for your Web site. Tasks help you manage your workflow by creating a "to do" list and allow you to hand out assignments to different people. The tasks that you create are completely up to you. You can assign different files to people for them to work on, have them conduct a legal review of your site, update different information, or verify hyperlinks within your Web. This organization of tasks is an essential feature when you are working on a Web site with several people (or even different groups of people) because it helps you ensure that all the necessary work gets done.

Figure 1-5: Inspect all your Web site's hyperlinks from the Hyperlinks view.

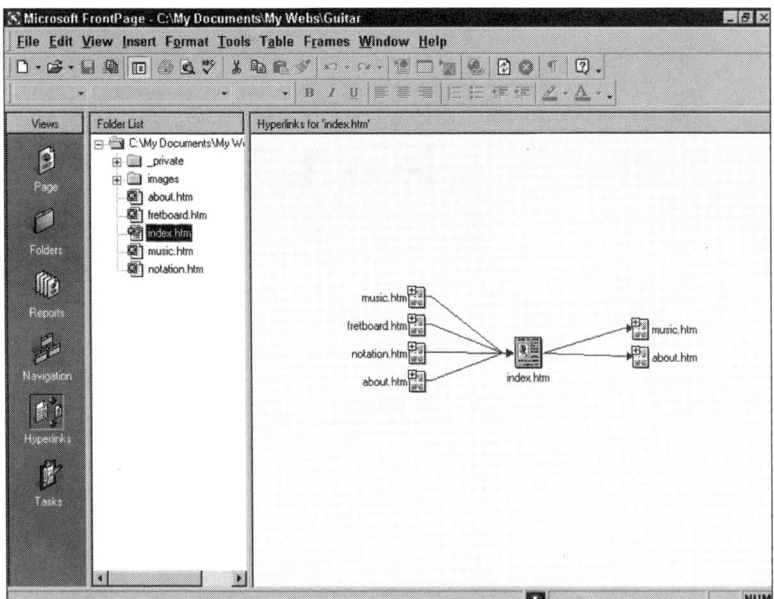

Getting Help

If you become stuck while working with FrontPage, you can refer to one of the many FrontPage help options. These options can answer most of your questions or help you find other resources.

- **Help⇨Microsoft FrontPage Help** opens the main help window, as shown in Figure 1-6. You can browse through the contents, enter questions for the Answer Wizard, or search the index for specific terms.

- **Help⇨What's This?** turns on context-sensitive help. When you move your mouse cursor over an object that has more information available, a question mark appears by the cursor. Left-click the object while the cursor has the question mark beside it to see the information.

Figure 1-6: The extensive help feature operates much like your other Windows applications.

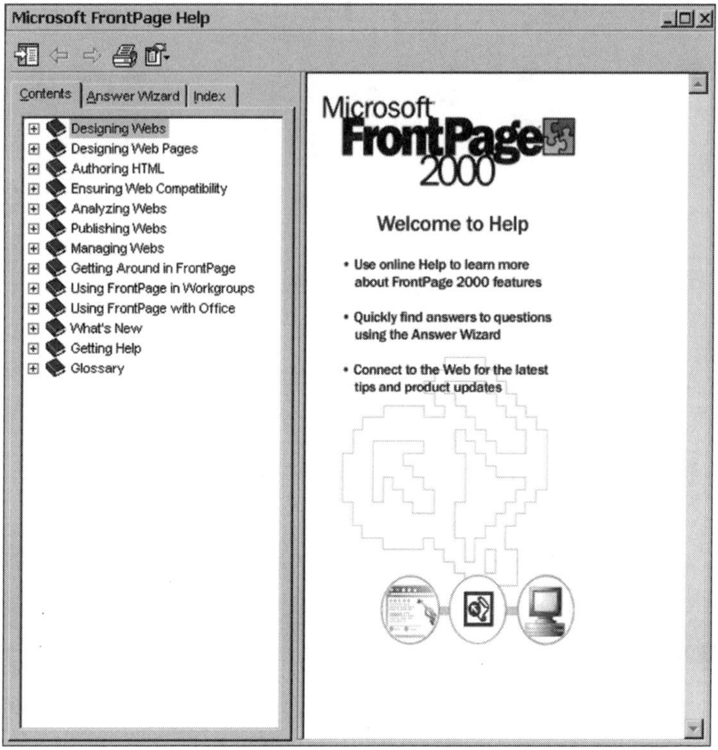

- **Help➪Office on the Web** launches your Web browser and connects you to the Microsoft Office Update Web site. You can download updates (if available) for Office 2000 applications and seek further assistance directly from Microsoft.

In addition to these help features, you can access ToolTips by moving your mouse cursor over many of the buttons, icons, and other objects in FrontPage. Tool tips are helpful reminders that explain the function of the item you are pointing at.

Now that you've become acquainted with the FrontPage main screens, you can start using FrontPage to create your first Web site!

CHAPTER 2
CREATING YOUR FIRST WEB SITE

IN THIS CHAPTER

- FrontPage creates Web sites *and* Web pages
- Planning your Web site before you create it
- Types of Web sites you can create with FrontPage
- Creating your first Web site with FrontPage

The World Wide Web is built with Web sites, or Webs, which are collections of Web pages linked together to form a tightly knit presentation of information, ideas, or services. You can use FrontPage to create personal sites that represent your views and enthusiasm for your interests or hobbies. By publishing your thoughts to the world, you may trigger a lively discussion with like-minded (or opposing, if you like) people. The sky is truly the limit!

In addition to personal Web sites, you can build business Web sites that advertise your goods and services to the world. Being online establishes a 24-hours a day, 7 days a week Internet presence that allows you to communicate with your customers easily. You can even conduct business through your Web site by offering online ordering and other services.

FrontPage closely integrates creating a Web site with creating the pages that go into the site. In this chapter, I show you how to plan and build a Web site that takes advantage of this site-and-page integration. By enabling you to create multiple Web pages that share a theme, FrontPage saves you time and lessens your frustration.

Planning Your Web Site

Before you run FrontPage and start creating your site, take some time to think about what you want to achieve through your Web site. The planning you do now will pay off in the long run. This section walks you through the five planning stages that I recommend. I used these steps to create the guitar Web site for this book. Maintaining focus is important to building a compelling Web site that attracts attention and successfully communicates your message to your visitors.

You can go through these same stages as you plan your own Web site — no matter what kind of site you decide to create. After you have your thoughts together about your subject, audience, goals, site layout, and Web server, you'll be able to create your site without forgetting anything or having to redo things midway through. Maintaining focus is important to building a compelling Web site that attracts attention and successfully communicates your message to your visitors.

Choose your subject

First, build your Web site around a subject you are interested in. Enthusiasm is contagious, and people who visit your site will see and react positively to the love and care you devote to your subject. Here are a few suggestions to spark your imagination:

- Create a site devoted to a hobby of yours, such as gardening or woodworking.

- Think of fun activities you enjoy, such as sports, movies, music, or games. Create a Web site to interact with others who share your passion or talents

- Do you have a social cause that you would like to promote, such as fighting cancer? Create a site about it to educate visitors and increase their awareness of the issue!

- If you are interested in local politics, you can create a site devoted to the issues and candidates that you endorse.

- Create a site to promote your business and advertise your goods or services online. Home business can really benefit from an online presence since you don't have a store for people to visit in person.

Because I'm learning how to play the guitar, I use that as my subject. It's fun, I enjoy it, and I want to share my experiences and knowledge with others.

Define your goals

Now that you have a subject in mind, ask yourself what you actually want to achieve with your Web site. Do you want to share your knowledge through an informative Web site or teach people how to do something? Do you want to promote a product, ideas, or person, such as a political candidate? Are you providing entertainment, offering services, or selling goods?

These goals, and others, aren't always mutually exclusive. You can have a Web site that informs *and* teaches, but you need to choose a primary focus. Your choice then helps you decide the format and style of the pages you add to your site. When you start laying out your site on paper, think about the kind of graphical theme, colors, and decorative pictures that support your goal.

My primary goal for the sample guitar site is to inform. I want to share some things I learned while teaching myself how to play the guitar, and include information ranging from how to hold a guitar to more advanced material on alternate tunings. This decision affects the kinds of Web pages I will add to my site when I start to build it. Because I am not selling anything, I don't have to worry about creating online order forms and conducting business transactions over the Web. Also, I'm not dealing with a serious subject such as cancer treatment, so I can feel free to include humor without offending anyone. Humor is in the eye of the beholder, however. Many subjects, even serious ones, can benefit from a light touch in places. Visitors to my Web site will (I hope) learn to enjoy the guitar as I have.

Target your audience

Another key factor in building an interesting Web site is defining your audience. You don't necessarily have to go out and conduct extensive market research, but you should consider the characteristics of the audience you want to communicate with. Your choice of audience ultimately boils down to deciding how broad or narrow an audience you are trying to appeal to. A few factors you should keep in mind are the following:

- **Age:** Is there a specific age group that you want to include or exclude? Is your subject matter appropriate or even appealing to children?

- **Style:** Your choice of a style or graphical theme will affect your audience. If your subject is lighthearted and fun, you can choose bright colors and whimsical pictures to decorate your site. On the other hand, you should take care not to offend people by treating more serious subjects too casually. FrontPage allows you to easily create a distinctive style for your Web site with ready-made themes, so you can quickly browse through different styles before making your final decision.

- **Technology:** Not everyone uses the latest version of the leading Web browsers. To reach the largest possible audience, avoid using the most advanced Web technologies, such as Cascading Style Sheets or Dynamic HTML. People who do not have a browser capable of using such late-breaking Web technologies will receive errors and may even crash their browser when they try to load your Web pages. The good news is that FrontPage allows you to decide what versions of the most popular Web browser to support as you create your site.

Given the goals I set for myself, I decided that the guitar site should appeal to people in their late teens and older, should have a classy but not overly serious style, and should use Web technologies that are compatible with most Web browsers (with possibly a few exceptions to make things interesting!).

Storyboard your site

Storyboarding is a simple brainstorming exercise that allows you to get your thoughts about your site down on paper in picture form. Take a blank piece of paper and start by drawing a *home page* at the top, which represents the first page of your site that people will visit. You can use boxes, circles, or anything you feel comfortable drawing. It doesn't have to be perfect; you just need to get your thoughts down on paper. Next, underneath your home page, draw other pages that will connect to your home page and name them according to the function they will serve in your Web site. Figure 2-1 shows my storyboard for the guitar Web site. Notice that I've connected my Web pages by lines. My storyboard shows where the pages will appear in the site and at what level.

I've divided my site into four main areas: information about guitars, music, links to other Web sites that I like, and information about me and the site I am creating. The instrument and music pages lead to more in-depth information that forms the bulk of my Web site. The links and site information pages will be small, but they are commonly used in Web sites. It's a good idea to give people who visit your site the benefit of your Web experience by pointing them to more information and sharing something about yourself and how you created your site.

Continue drawing your Web and filling in Web pages until you've formed a good game plan for your site.

Figure 2-1: Draw your Web site on paper as you brainstorm its content and layout.

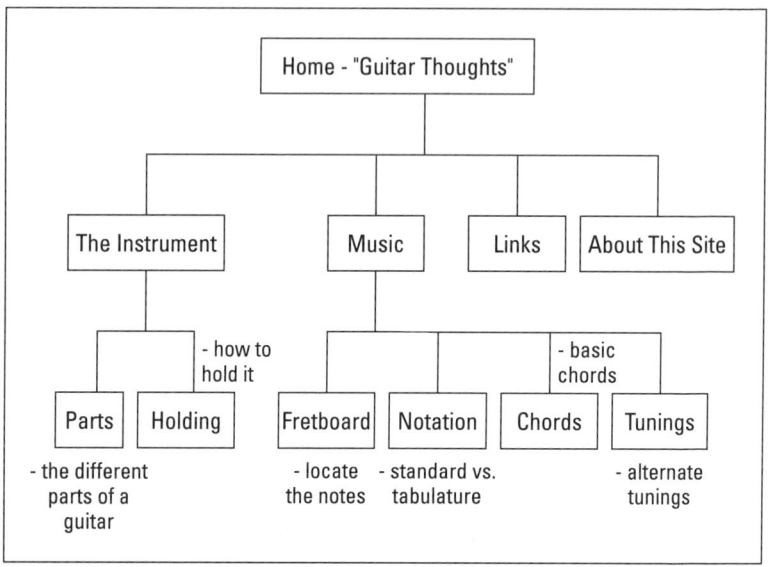

Find a Web server

The last step in Web planning is making sure that you have a Web server to store your site when you are ready to publish it. As you create your site, you store it on your hard drive, but you must save it to a Web server before you can view it on the Internet. Web servers are computers that are connected to the Internet, usually with permanent connections. Servers enable people to see the Web pages stored on their hard drives. Probably the best thing to do is to contact your Internet Service Provider (ISP). Most ISPs offer free Web hosting services (for non-commercial Web sites), help you save your Web site to their server, and tell you your site's Web address. However, expect them to limit the amount of space your site can occupy and the amount of monthly traffic your Web site can generate.

Chapter 2: Creating Your First Web Site

You must save your Web site to a Web server when you are finished creating it so that people can view it on the Internet. If you don't want to use your ISP, plenty of companies out there, such as GeoCities, Angelfire, and Xoom, offer free Web hosting services.

Creating Your First Web Site

Creating your Web site with FrontPage is fast and easy! You can create many types of Webs in FrontPage by using Web *templates* or *wizards,* which do much of the work for you. Templates are preformatted Webs that may contain Web pages (the actual number depends on your choice of Web) already named and formatted for you. This is like creating a new document, such as a report or memo, using a Microsoft Word template. Wizards step you through the process of creating a new Web by having you answer several questions that set the types of pages for you.

You can automatically create eight types of Webs with FrontPage. Five of these Webs are made by using templates:

- **One Page Web:** A single, blank Web page.

- **Customer Support Web:** Designed to help you provide customer support services through your Web.

- **Empty Web:** A new Web with no content.

- **Personal Web:** A Web site that is appropriate for personal interests.

- **Project Web:** A Web with features that make working on a project with others easier.

Three of the eight Webs are made by using wizards:

- **Corporate Presence Wizard:** Creates a professional, business-related Web.
- **Discussion Web Wizard:** Creates a discussion Web for people to share ideas.
- **Import Web Wizard:** Opens an existing Web into FrontPage.

I create a One Page Web in this book and fill it with my own information, but the Web site and Web page topics you read about in this book are applicable to all the different types of Webs.

Follow these steps to create your Web:

1. If you don't have it running, launch FrontPage by clicking the Start button and then choosing Programs➪Microsoft FrontPage.

2. Select File➪New➪Web. Figure 2-2 shows the New Web dialog box that appears.

3. Click the One Page Web icon in the left part of the dialog box. This option creates a new Web site with one page, your home page.

4. Specify the location of the Web on your hard drive by entering a folder name, such as Guitar, in the Options area of the dialog box.

5. Click OK to have FrontPage create your new Web site.

Chapter 2: Creating Your First Web Site   **25**

Figure 2-2:   Select the One Page Web icon and provide a folder name to create your One Page Web.

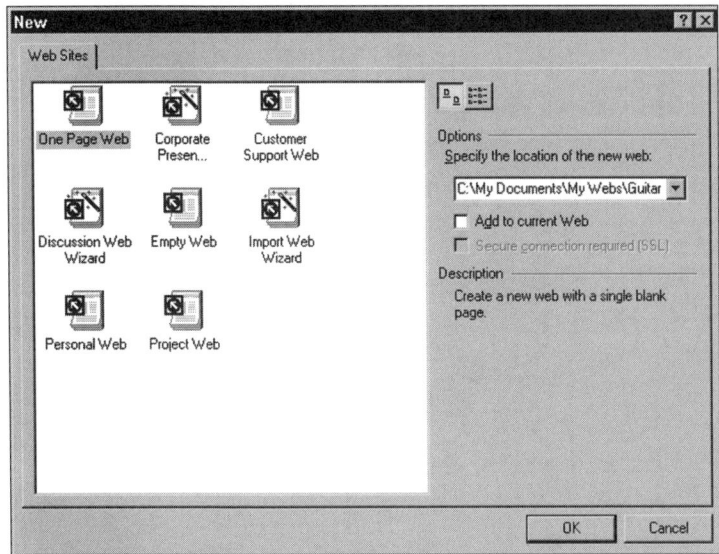

When FrontPage creates your Web, it changes to the Page view and opens a new, blank Web page. Although this page isn't part of your site yet, go ahead and experiment. Type in something to see what it's like. It's fun!

If you switch to the Navigation view, as shown in Figure 2-3, you can see that FrontPage has created your new Web with a home page. Take a peek at the Folder list beside the Navigation view main window. These are the files and folders that belong to your new Web site.

FrontPage stores the Webs you create in C:\My Documents\My Webs\ by default. Unless you have an overriding reason to store your Webs somewhere else, stick with this setting. That way, you can easily find your Webs on your computer.

Figure 2-3: A new FrontPage Web has been born and is ready for you to customize.

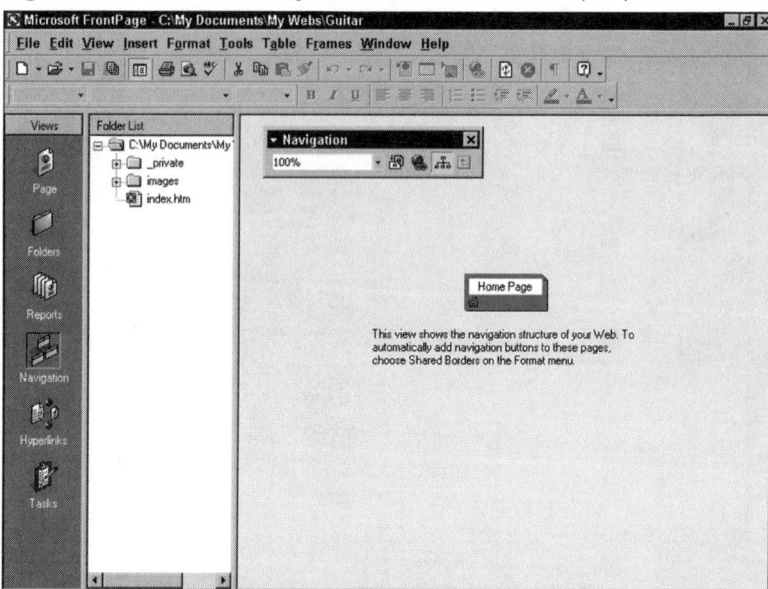

Working with Your New Web

Those who dreamed up FrontPage specifically designed it for you to work with Web sites, not merely Web pages. Therefore, as you work in FrontPage, you will open, close, and possibly delete entire Web sites. Because a site does not consist of just one file, FrontPage has special menu items for you to use to accomplish these tasks.

Closing and opening your Web

If you are done working with your Web, you should close it like any other document.

Close your FrontPage Web by selecting File→Close Web. FrontPage prompts you to save any Web pages that have been modified and then closes the Web. If you want to open another Web, select File➪Open Web and then select a Web folder that is stored on your hard drive. Click Open to open your Web. Figure 2-4 shows the Open Web dialog box. Notice that the Web folder has a unique icon that differentiates it from the other folders on your hard drive. This folder looks like a normal Windows Explorer folder but has a tiny globe inside it.

If you are working with a few Webs consistently, use the File➪Recent Webs menu. FrontPage stores the names of the last four Webs you worked on for easy retrieval.

Figure 2-4: Choose File➪Open Web, select a Web folder, and then click OK to open a Web.

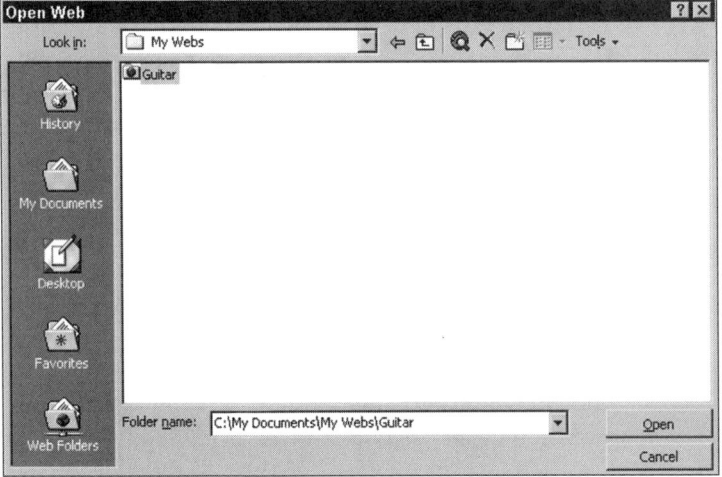

Opening your home page

Opening your Web site is the first step in accessing your Web pages so that you can work on them. After you open your Web site, you can open the individual Web pages. Follow these steps to open your home page:

1. Make sure that you have FrontPage running and have opened your Web site.
2. Switch to the Navigation view by clicking the Navigation icon from the Views bar.
3. Double-click your home page (it's the box that says Home Page) in the main Navigation view window to open it.

You should open your Web site first and then open the pages you wish to work on.

Saving your work

You should always save your work. Try to make a habit of saving every few minutes or whenever you make several changes to a Web page. Switch to Page view if you are not already there and make sure that your home page is open. Go ahead and type something in so that the page has changes in it; then click the Save icon in the Standard toolbar. FrontPage then saves your page.

You should save your work often. Take it from me: Nothing is more frustrating than spending hours creating something really wonderful, only to lose it all when your program or computer crashes. Although FrontPage is largely stable and bug free, FrontPage itself doesn't have to crash for you to lose your work.

Closing your home page

After you've opened up your home page to either look it over or make changes, you'll need to eventually close it. If you've made any changes to your home page, you'll want to save it first, as outlined in the previous section. If you forget to save your file first, don't worry. FrontPage prompts you to save any changes before it lets you close a page. All that's left for you to do is select File⇨Close from the Main menu, and FrontPage will close your home page.

Deleting an unwanted Web

If you want to delete your Web and start over from scratch, switch to the Folders view by selecting Folders in the Views bar. Then right-click the topmost folder, which is your Web site. Select Delete and then choose Delete this Web entirely. Click OK to delete the Web. Figure 2-5 shows the Confirm Delete dialog box that appears when you choose to delete a Web.

Figure 2-5: Delete a Web by right-clicking the Web folder in the Folder list and then choosing Delete.

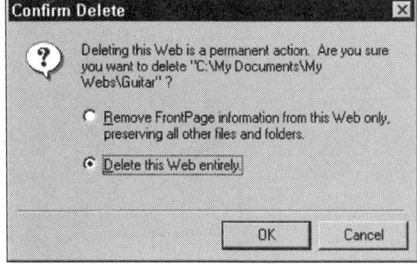

When you delete a Web in this manner, the action can't be undone.

CHAPTER 3
WORKING WITH YOUR WEB PAGES

IN THIS CHAPTER

- Entering text in your home page
- Aligning and formatting text
- Deleting material
- Previewing your work

If you have worked with a word processor before, you already have many of the skills required to complete the tasks presented in this chapter. This is one of the nicest features of FrontPage: You can use knowledge that you have gained working with other Microsoft Office programs and immediately put it to use in FrontPage.

In this chapter, I show you how to perform the basic tasks you will need to accomplish while working with your Web pages. You'll be able to open your Web pages to work on them, enter, align, and format text, delete material, preview your work, and save your work when you are finished. All these tasks are important because you'll use them with almost every Web page you create.

Opening Your Web Pages

Of course, you have to open your Web pages in order to work with them. Without further ado, follow these steps:

1. Launch FrontPage by clicking the Start button and then choosing Programs⇨Microsoft FrontPage.

Chapter 3: Working with Your Web Pages   **31**

2. Open your Web site by selecting File➪Open➪Web and choose your Web. If you want to start from scratch, choose File➪New➪Web and select the kind of Web you want.

3. Switch to the Navigation view by clicking the Navigation View icon from the Views bar.

4. Double-click a Web page in the main Navigation view window to open it.

You can have more than one Web page open when you are working. Try going back to the Navigation view and double-clicking more of your pages. They will open and be displayed in the Page view. If you want to switch between pages while you are working, choose the Window menu and select a different Web page.

You should open your Web site first and then open the pages you want to work on.

Adding Text to Your Home Page

Although multimedia is all the rage on the Web, text is still the easiest way to present your ideas to the world. Text doesn't take much time to enter and it loads a lot faster than graphics or multimedia components over the Internet.

Entering and editing text

To enter text in your Web pages, place your cursor in your page by clicking; then begin typing. Your cursor appears as a blinking vertical bar. Continue typing words, sentences, and paragraphs as you would in a word processor. Press Enter to start a new paragraph. You can use your arrow keys to move your cursor around your page or click your left mouse button to move your text insertion point.

Cutting, copying, and pasting text

As you work with your Web page, you may need to move some text around after you've typed it. Follow these steps to cut, copy, and paste text:

1. Highlight the text by clicking your left mouse button at the beginning of a word, sentence, or paragraph and holding your mouse button down. Drag the mouse to the end of the text you want to select and then release your mouse button.

2. Click either the cut or copy icon on the FrontPage Standard toolbar, as shown in Figure 3-1. (Cutting text removes it from your Page and stores it in your clipboard so that you can paste it later. Copying text just stores a copy in your clipboard.)

3. If you want to paste what you just cut or copied, move your cursor to the location where you want to paste it and click the Paste button on the Standard toolbar.

Figure 3-1: The Standard toolbar makes carrying out commands easy.

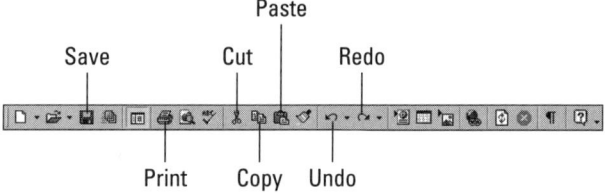

You can align text on your Web pages in a variety of ways, all of which are similar to the common text alignment features in most word processors.

Aligning text to the left, right, or center

Place your cursor inside a line or paragraph of text and then click one of these alignment buttons from the FrontPage Formatting toolbar (see Figure 3-2):

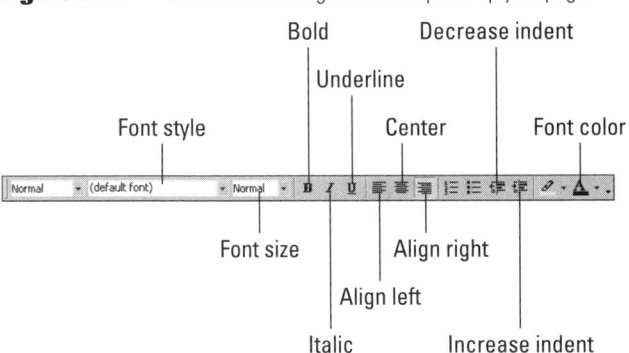

Figure 3-2: Use the Formatting toolbar to spruce up your page.

- Font style
- Bold
- Underline
- Center
- Decrease indent
- Font color
- Font size
- Align left
- Align right
- Italic
- Increase indent

- **Align left:** Aligns your text flush with the left margin of your Web page.

- **Center:** Centers text on your Web page.

- **Align right:** Aligns your text flush with the right margin of your Web page, leaving the left margin "ragged," or unaligned.

Indenting text

Extra *white space,* or empty space around items on a Web page, often makes the page more readable for a visitor. Place your mouse cursor anywhere in the paragraph that you want to indent and click the Increase Indent button from the Formatting toolbar. Your text will automatically be indented, as shown in Figure 3-3. Notice that I have increased the indentation of the main paragraphs on my home page.

Figure 3-3: Indenting is an easy way to increase the amount of empty space around your text.

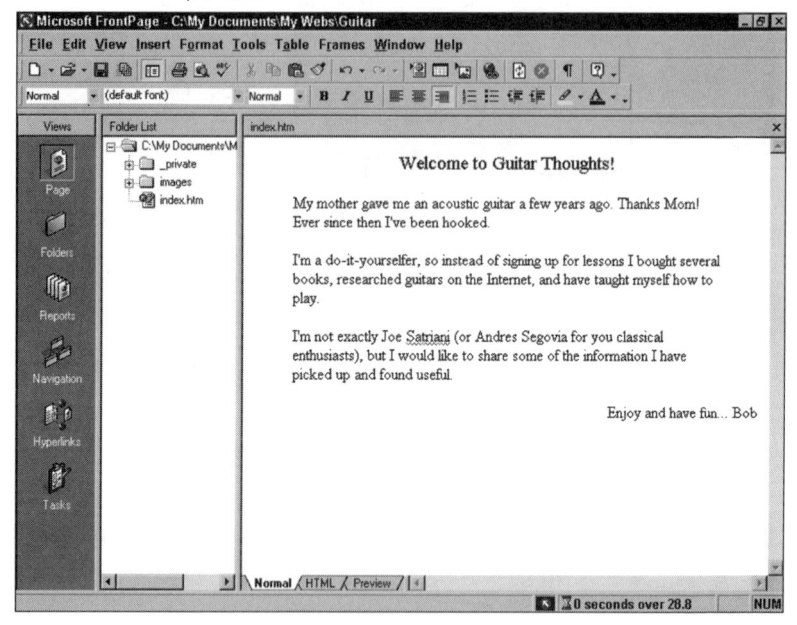

If you want to decrease the amount a paragraph is indented, click the Decrease Indent button.

Formatting Your Text

Formatting involves changing the font of your text, making it bold, choosing a different color, or changing its style. Most of the text-formatting features are identical to those found in Microsoft Word.

Changing text font and size

Place your mouse cursor where you want the new font to begin and then select a new font from the pull-down Font menu on the Formatting toolbar, as shown in Figure 3-4. Notice that I'm choosing Arial for my heading — Arial makes a good header font and is installed on most systems. You can change the size the same way.

Figure 3-4: Choose different fonts exactly as you would in a word processing program, but be careful.

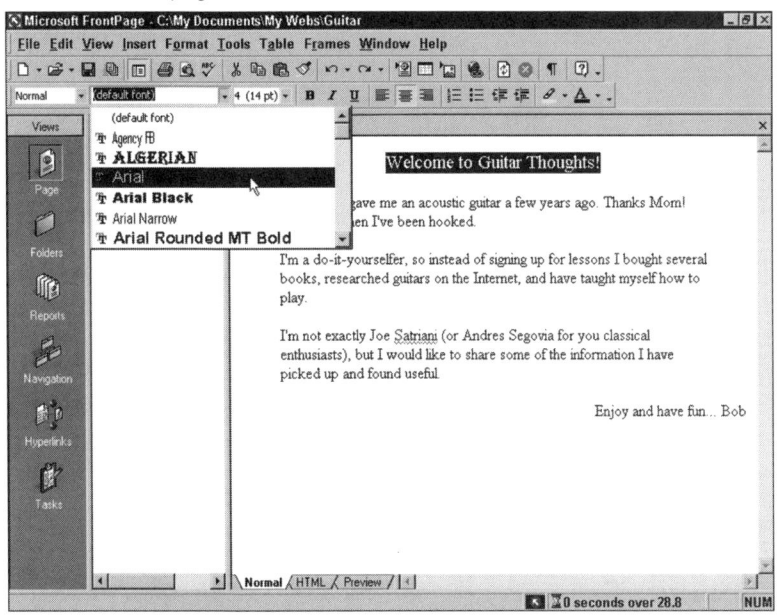

Be careful when you choose different fonts. If people viewing your Web pages don't have the font you chose installed on their computer, the page will not look the way you intend it.

Making text underlined, bold, or italicized

First, use your mouse to highlight the text you want to underline, make bold, or italicize; then click one of these buttons from the Formatting toolbar:

- **Bold:** Makes your text stand out and look **heavy**.

- **Italic:** *Italicizes* your text and generally connotes a special meaning or emphasis.

- **Underline:** <u>Underlines</u> your text for extra emphasis. Be careful when you choose to underline text on a Web page. Hyperlinks are normally displayed as underlined text, and you may confuse people into thinking you are trying to link to another Web page when you underline a word or passage of text.

Choosing different colors for your text

Changing the color of your text emphasizes it and makes it stand out from the rest of your Web page. Use your mouse to highlight the text you want to change and then click the down arrow next to the Font Color button on your Formatting toolbar. Doing so opens the Font Color dialog box, as shown in Figure 3-5. This allows you to change the color of the text you have selected.

Figure 3-5: Text stands out from the rest of your Web page when you make it a different color.

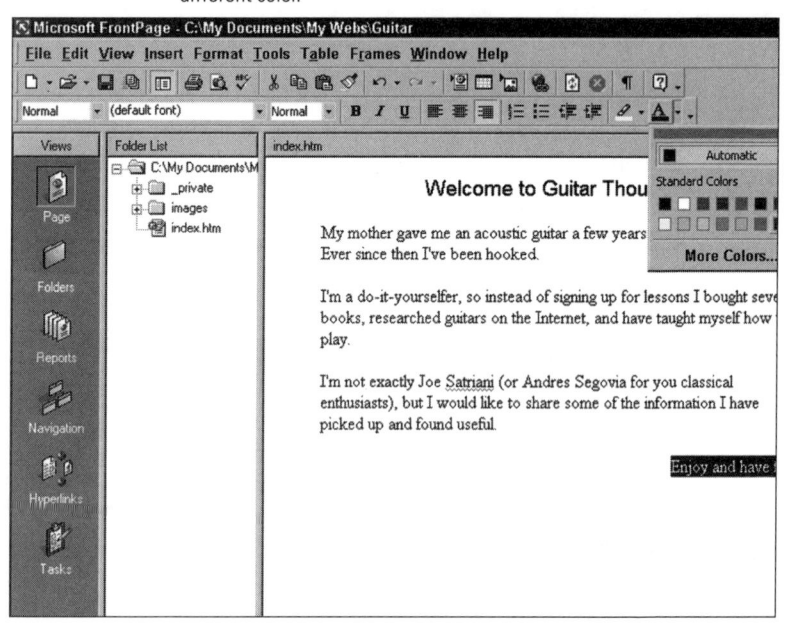

Deleting Material

Some of the Web templates FrontPage puts at your disposal may automatically include material you're not too interested in keeping. Depending on what material you are removing, you may wish to delete it the following ways:

- **Text:** Highlight the text you want to delete and press Delete.

- **Pictures and other objects:** Place your cursor just after the object you want to delete and press Backspace.

> **Tip:** FrontPage has Undo and Redo features just like the other Office programs. If you make a mistake and accidentally delete something, click the Undo button on the Standard toolbar. (If you undo too much work, don't panic. Just click the Redo button and FrontPage will change your Web page back one step.)

Previewing Your Work

Although you can see how your Web pages will look while you are editing them, previewing your work periodically is a very good idea. You can use two methods of viewing your Web pages in a non-editing mode: previewing them in FrontPage and loading them into your Web browser.

Previewing in FrontPage

You can preview your Web pages and your Web site within FrontPage. First, switch to Page view. If you already have one or more Web pages open, choose one from the Window menu and then click the Preview tab in the lower portion of the Page view window. FrontPage, as shown in Figure 3-6, then previews your Web page as it will look in a Web browser.

> While you are previewing your page, all the links are active just as they would be on the Internet. If you click one — even an internal link — FrontPage will connect to that Web page. These active links make checking your entire site a breeze because you can start from your home page and follow all your links.

Figure 3-6: Previewing your pages in FrontPage is like loading them into a Web browser to test them.

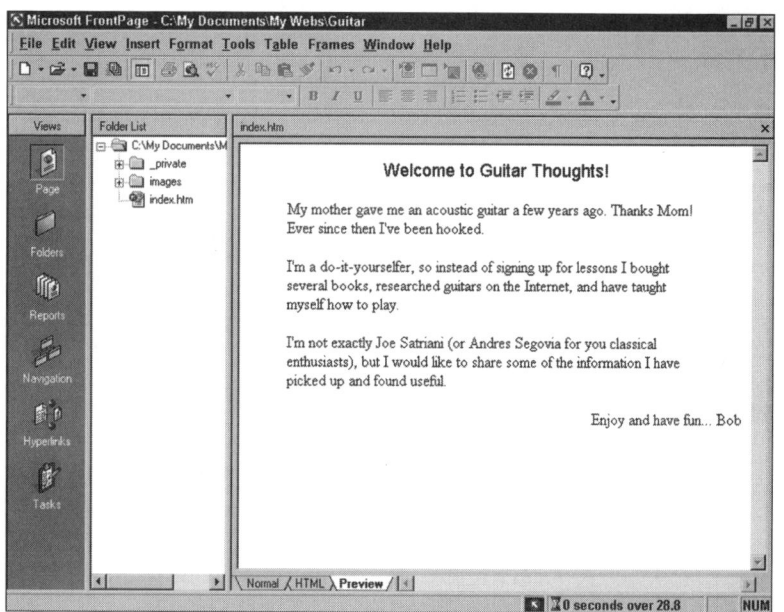

Previewing in your Web browser

If you want to see your work in an actual Web browser, simply select File➪Preview in Browser. This option opens the Preview in Browser dialog box, as shown in Figure 3-7, where you can choose a Web browser installed on your computer. After you select a browser and a window size and then click Preview, FrontPage launches your Web browser and loads your Web page automatically.

CHAPTER 4
CUSTOMIZING YOUR WEB SITE

IN THIS CHAPTER

- Add Web pages to your site
- Give your Web a snazzy, consistent look
- Create shared borders and navigation bars

Whenever you create a new Web site using FrontPage templates (a One Page Web or Personal Web template, for example), FrontPage creates a new site and automatically generates one or more new Web pages for you.

Now you can start turning this boilerplate into something you can call your own! In this chapter, I show you how to customize your new Web site. Remember, it's *your* Web site, not FrontPage's. The planning material you created in Chapter 2 will help you in this process.

Adding More Web Pages to Your Site

Up to this point, you've just worked with your home page. That's a good start, but you probably want to add more Web pages to fill out your site.

> **Tip:** Have your storyboard handy to make your job easier. You are essentially trying to recreate your storyboard in the Navigation view.

Chapter 3: Working with Your Web

Figure 3-7: You can preview your work in any Web browser you have your computer.

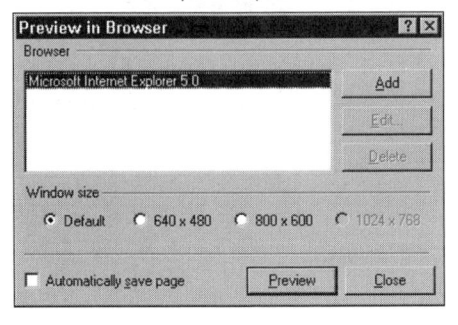

Chapter 4: Customizing Your Web Site   **41**

Adding New Web Pages

Adding new Web pages is easy. Switch to the Navigation view by clicking the Navigation View icon and following these steps:

1. Right-click in the blank area of the Folders List window. Doing so opens a context-sensitive menu with three options: New Page, New Folder, and Paste.

2. Choose New page. A new file will appear in the Folders list, and FrontPage assigns it a default name, such as new_page_1.htm.

3. The new page's name is highlighted and there's a box around it. This means you can enter your filename now. Refer to your storyboard so that you give the proper name to the correct pages.

Tip: When you name your files, give them a name that makes sense and reflects the contents of the Web page. I can tell by looking at About.htm, for example, that it is a Web page with information about this Web site.

Remember: You should make sure that your new files have an .htm extension. Otherwise, they will not load into a Web browser.

Tip: If you make a mistake when you name your file, you can delete it (select the file and press your Delete key) or right-click the file, choose Rename, and enter the new name.

Making your new pages part of your Web

After you create your new Web pages, you must add each new page to your site in the Navigation view. By doing so, you let FrontPage know where all your new pages fit into your site. FrontPage uses this information to create navigation bars. (See the section "Adding Shared Borders and Navigation Buttons," later in this chapter, for more information on navigation bars.)

Here's how you add a new page to your site:

1. Switch to the Navigation view by clicking the Navigation View icon; then select a Web page that you have just created in the Folder list window. When you select it, hold down your left mouse button.

2. Drag the file over to the main Navigation view window, as shown in Figure 4-1, and keep your left mouse button pressed. Notice that as you drag your Web page, dynamic "rubber band lines" automatically appear in the Navigation view to show you where the page will fit into the structure of your site when you decide to release your mouse button. Because this is the first new page you're adding, the only place it can go is "under" your home page.

   After you create more new pages, experiment by dragging them to different parts of your site and see how the Navigation view changes. The Navigation view is somewhat like an organizational chart of a company. It shows the boss at the top (your home page) and different levels of people (your other pages) underneath. Each new sublevel can have one or more Web pages assigned to it.

3. Drop (release your left mouse button) the Web page when you are satisfied with its location.

Adding individual Web pages is easy, but don't forget to make them a part of your site in Navigation view. If you don't, they won't show up in any of the navigation buttons or links that FrontPage creates for you.

Figure 4-1: Dragging a new Web page into the Navigation view adds the page to your site.

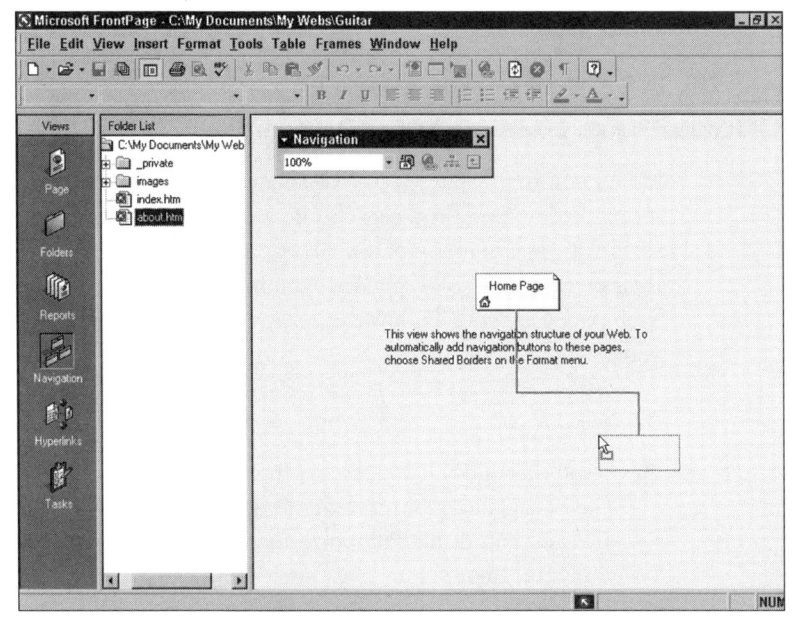

Giving your new pages titles

The next step is to give each new Web page a title. The title is what shows up in the Title Bar of a Web browser when a person loads that Web page. It's important to have clear titles for your Web pages so that people know exactly where they are in your site and the purpose of the Web page they are viewing. Try not to use long sentences when a word or two will do the job. To add titles, perform the following steps for each of your new pages:

1. While in the Navigation view, select a Web page in the main Navigation view window.

2. Select the File➪Properties menu.

3. In the Title field, enter a title that matches the purpose of your Web page and click OK.

CliffsNotes Creating Your First Web Site with FrontPage 2000

Although your new title doesn't show up in the Navigation view, don't worry. When people load your page into their Web browser, the title appears in the Title Bar of their browser.

Choosing a Theme for Your Web

When you first create your Web site, your Web pages might look a little bland. You can choose a theme for your site to spruce it up. Themes are unified graphical designs that have their own unique color schemes, graphics, buttons, and other Web page elements. Follow these steps to choose a theme for your Web:

1. Select Format⇨Theme from the menu bar.

2. Scroll through the themes presented in the list on the left side of the dialog box shown in Figure 4-2 until you find one that you think will look good and is appropriate for your site. I happen to like Postmodern.

Figure 4-2: Select a theme from the list and see it previewed in the main window of this dialog box.

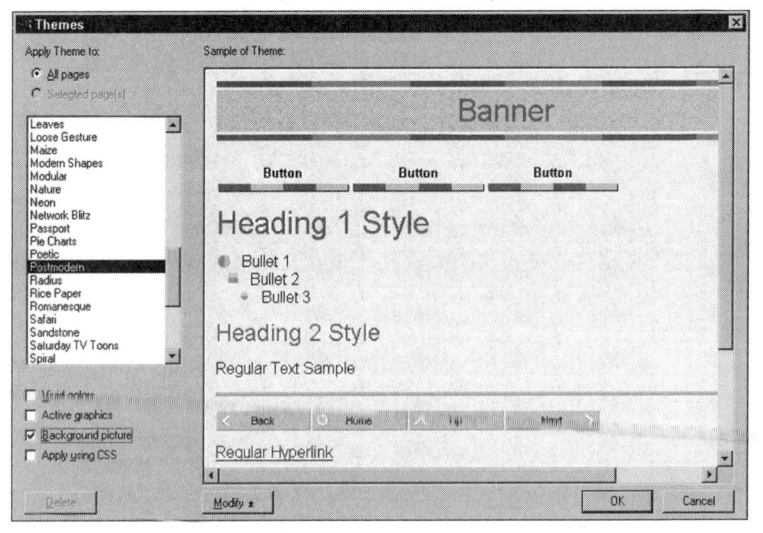

3. Leave the Apply Theme to All pages button selected, because you are applying this theme to the entire Web site. Later, if you want to change the theme for one page, you can come back to this dialog box and select Apply Theme to This page.

4. Select one or more of the other options below the list of themes. If you want to see the effect these options have, click the option button to turn it on or off. The preview window will update so that you can see the difference. Your options are as follows:

   - **Vivid Colors:** Makes the color scheme of the theme more vibrant. Experiment with this option and look closely at the preview window to see what changes.

   - **Active Graphics:** Uses animated graphics for bullets and buttons that change appearance when you move your mouse over them. Choose this option only if you aren't worried about the limitations of older Web browsers. Active graphics use advanced techniques behind the scenes to achieve their effects, and they may prove too high-powered for some of the older Web browsers out there.

   - **Background Picture:** Applies a tiled background texture to your Web pages. I recommend choosing this option. White (or other solid color backgrounds) look nice in a professional or business Web site, but for my Guitar site, I want something a little more interesting.

   - **Apply Using CSS:** Creates styles for text elements in your Web page using Cascading Style Sheets. This option should be chosen only if you are not concerned about supporting older Web browsers. Many older browsers do not support CSS. Without getting too technical, CSS gives you more formatting power and flexibility than conventional HTML, and strives to separate the structural organization (the strict role of HTML) from the presentational formatting (such as making text bold or italicized) of a Web page.

5. When you are finished, click OK. FrontPage churns for a few seconds as it applies all the different theme elements to your Web pages, and then — voilà! — your Web site has a new coat of paint!

Adding Shared Borders and Navigation Buttons

It's time to unleash a little more FrontPage magic on your Web by adding shared borders and navigation buttons. Shared borders are real timesavers because they create well-defined areas, or borders, that all your Web pages will display.

You can create a shared border on the bottom of your pages and put your name, e-mail address, and copyright information in it. You can also use shared borders to show the name of each page at the top of the screen. All your pages will display the shared borders and you have to enter the information only once.

Some shared borders can also have navigation buttons, which are grouped together in a navigation bar. Navigation bars are links to the pages of your Web site that FrontPage automatically creates for you. For example, you can create a navigation bar at the top of your site with all the main Web pages represented by buttons. Someone simply clicks a button and that Web page loads into his or her browser. This feature saves you time and effort, too. After you choose a navigation structure, every Web page that you add to your site in the Navigation view is automatically present in the navigation bars.

Follow these steps to add shared borders and a navigation bar:

1. Make sure that your Web is open; then open your home page and switch to the Page view.

2. Right-click in the main Page view window. Doing so opens a context-sensitive menu with several options.

3. Choose Shared Borders, which opens the Shared Borders dialog box, as shown in Figure 4-3.

Figure 4-3: Add shared borders and a navigation bar to all your pages.

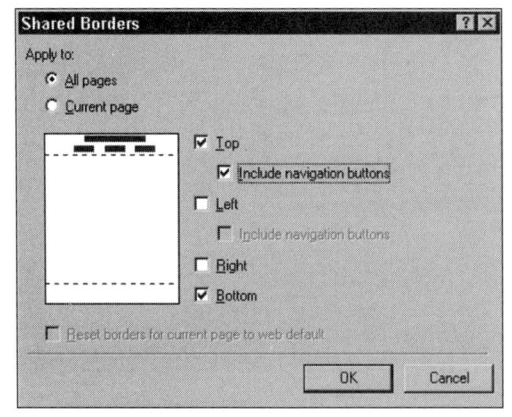

4. Select Apply to All pages if you want all the Web pages in your site to share the border you are adding.

5. Select a shared border to create. You can choose Top, Left, Right, or Bottom. Notice that the small preview window shows you where the borders will be on your Web pages.

6. Select the Include navigation buttons option in the Top shared border.

7. Click OK when you are done. This action closes the Shared Borders dialog box, and FrontPage creates the borders and navigation bar for you.

FrontPage returns to the Page view, and you can see several changes to your home page, as shown in Figure 4-4.

Figure 4-4: The shared borders are at the top and bottom; the page banner is inside the top border.

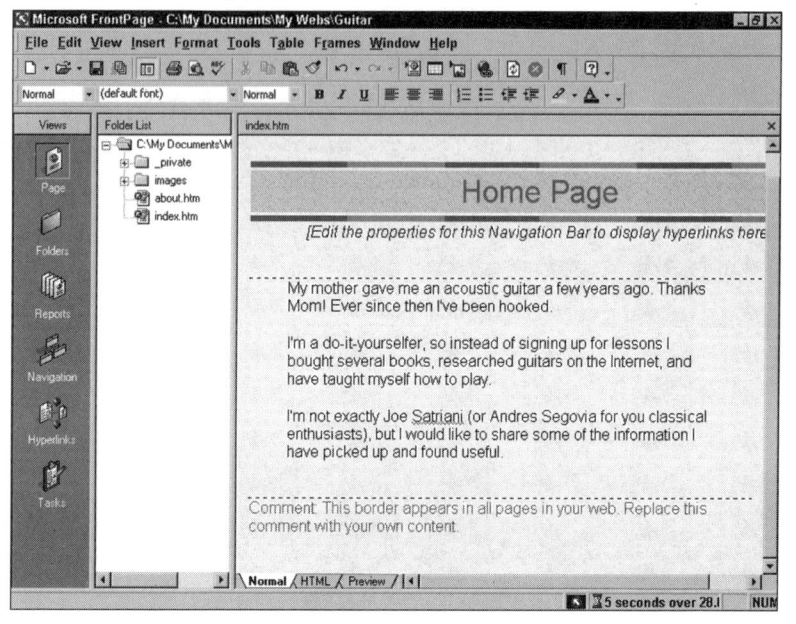

First and most obvious, you see a huge banner across the top of your page with the words *Home Page* inside it. This banner is called a *page banner*. Page banners are the program's way of showing the name of a Web page. This name will show up in all the navigation features that FrontPage uses. Everything above the dashed line at the top of the page is actually part of the top shared border.

Next, look down at the bottom of the page (I've taken out the heading and another line so that you can see it all in one figure). Everything below this second dashed line is in the bottom shared border. You can also see a comment in the bottom shared border. FrontPage uses this comment to remind you that you have a shared border. The comment won't show up in a Web browser (click the Preview tab to see how it disappears).

Chapter 4: Customizing Your Web Site

In the next three sections, I work from the top of your page down, changing the page banner, navigation bar, and shared border.

Naming your new Web pages

Rather than accept the name that FrontPage offers for your Web page, you should edit the page banner and give it its own name. Instead of *Home Page*, I want visitors to my site to see *Guitar Thoughts* in the page banner of my home page.

Follow these steps to name your pages and change the page banner:

1. Open a Web page in the Page view.

2. Double-click the page banner (the top colored box on the page). It has the current name of the Web page inside it.

3. After the Page Banner Properties dialog box appears, enter your new name for this Web page in the Page banner text field, as shown in Figure 4-5.

4. Click OK when you are finished. FrontPage updates the page banner and now displays your text.

Figure 4-5: Your new Web page name will appear in the page banner and in the navigation bars.

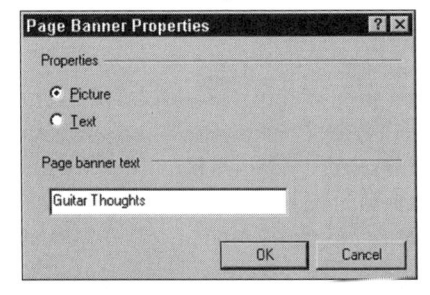

Working with navigation bars

Refer to Figure 4-4. Do you see the comment under the page banner? This is a placeholder for the navigation bar. It's empty until you add navigation buttons, which collectively make up the navigation bar. Follow these steps to add navigation buttons to your navigation bar:

1. Open a Web page in the Page view.

2. Double-click the comment below the page banner to open the Navigation Bar Properties dialog box, shown in Figure 4-6.

Figure 4-6: The Navigation Bar Properties dialog box is where you control what pages are used in your navigation bars.

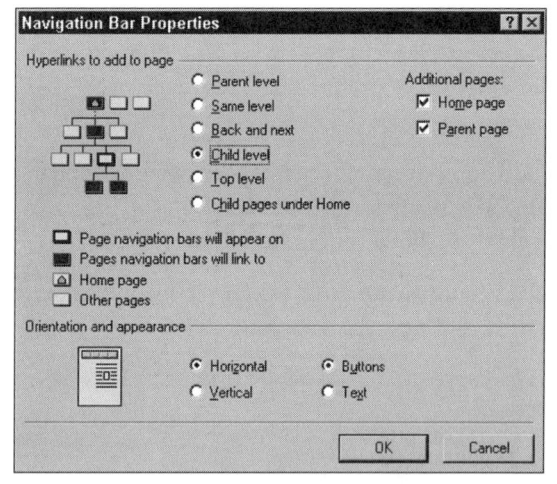

3. Next to the tiny Web site (made up of boxes) is a list of relationships that define the buttons you can display on each page. When you select a relationship, the Web site on the left side of the dialog box changes to show you which pages will be included in your navigation bar if you decide on that option. Next to this list are two additional pages that you can include in your navigation bar.

Chapter 4: Customizing Your Web Site

4. Choose the settings at the bottom of the dialog box to change the navigation bar orientation (horizontal or vertical) and appearance (buttons or text). In my Guitar site example, I've chosen to include the child pages (those pages underneath a page when you look at the site in Navigation view), the home page, and the parent page. Including these pages gives a visitor to my site plenty of options to go where they want and identify where they are.

5. When you have made your choices, click OK to close the Navigation Bar Properties dialog box. FrontPage makes all the changes to your Web site and takes you back to the Page view. Figure 4-7 shows how my site looks.

Figure 4-7: The navigation bar provides links to the pages in your site.

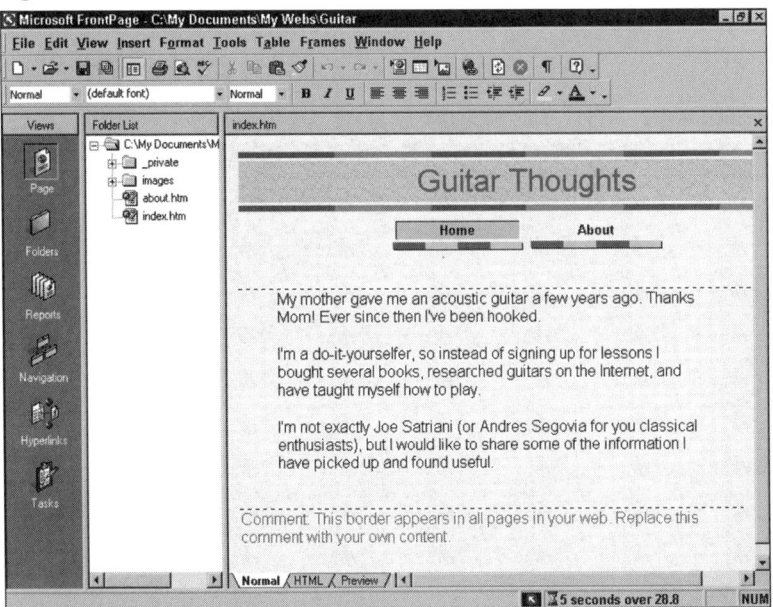

Working with shared borders

If you continue down the page, you see another shared border at the bottom that you created earlier. In this area, you can add information that will be displayed in all your pages. You can enter text, pictures, and anything else you can have on a Web page in a shared border. The only difference is that you enter it once and it is displayed on all the pages of your site.

> **Tip**
> You can delete the comment in the lower border if you like. If you need to come back and add or edit material, click the area where the shared border is located in the Page view to select the shared border. After you do so, a box will appear around the border, and you can enter whatever you like.

Type something in your lower shared border to see how it works. In Figure 4-8, I've added copyright information and my name and then centered the text on the line. You can format this text just like any other text you put in your Web page.

Figure 4-8: Click in the shared border and add your own material.

Chapter 4: Customizing Your Web Site

To finish, I decided to take a look at my home page in my Web browser, Microsoft Internet Explorer 5. Figure 4-9 shows how my site looks now with a navigation bar and a shared bottom border. Notice that the comments in the shared bottom border appear to be gone. They are actually still there; it's just that Web browsers know not to display comments.

Figure 4-9: Previewing my page in Internet Explorer.

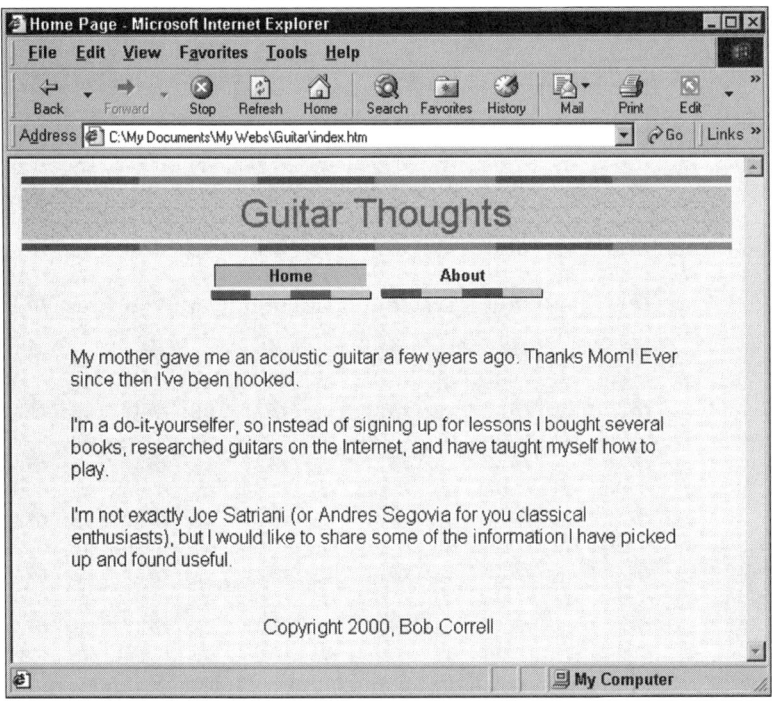

CHAPTER 5
BEEFING UP YOUR WEB PAGES WITH LINKS, LISTS, AND PICTURES

IN THIS CHAPTER

- Linking to other Web sites
- Creating e-mail links
- Adding lists to your Web pages
- Inserting pictures in your Web pages

It's time to learn how to add some fun stuff to your Web pages. Don't worry. Adding fun stuff is actually kind of fun because FrontPage makes it very easy for you to liven up your text-only Web pages with lots of eye-poppin' features. In this chapter, for example, I show you how easy it is to add hyperlinks, lists, and pictures to your Web pages.

Remember: Don't think that all this eye-candy is just empty calories. Besides breaking the monotony of plain 'ol text, your addition of links, lists, and pictures make your site much more visually appealing. When you add these elements to your Web pages, you'll create much more informative, interesting, and interactive Web pages.

Linking Web Pages

Although navigation bars do a pretty good job of linking your Web pages, they don't link your site to anything external. In other words, if you decide that you want to provide a link to Amazon.com so that people can search for books about guitars, you have to put that link in on your own. In addition, you may want to provide your own internal Web site links rather than rely exclusively on the FrontPage navigation bars. Either way, adding links to your Web pages is a snap.

Links are composed of two parts. The first part is what you actually see displayed in the Web page. The second part of a link is the destination address.

Creating links to external sites

You can provide links to any other Web site on the Internet if you wish, but narrowing your links list down to sites that relate to the topic your site covers is a good idea. For the guitar Web site, I chose to create an entire Web page devoted to interesting links that I think people would like to visit. By doing some legwork, I found these sites on my own and bookmarked them in my Web browser so that I wouldn't forget them. Later, when I created my Links page, I called the pages up into my Web browser and copied the Web addresses over to FrontPage. Follow these steps to add your own links in your Web page:

 1. Launch FrontPage, open your Web site, and open a Web page in the Page view.

 2. Enter text in your Web page to form the first part of the link. This text may be the name of the Web site you are linking to or some other convenient reminder.

3. Highlight the word or phrase you want to turn into a link with your mouse and then click the Hyperlink button (it looks like a little globe with a chain link below it) on the toolbar. Doing so opens the Create Hyperlink dialog box, as shown in Figure 5-1.

4. Enter the Web address of the Web page you want to be the destination of the link.

Figure 5-1: Make sure that you enter the correct Web address; otherwise, the link will not work.

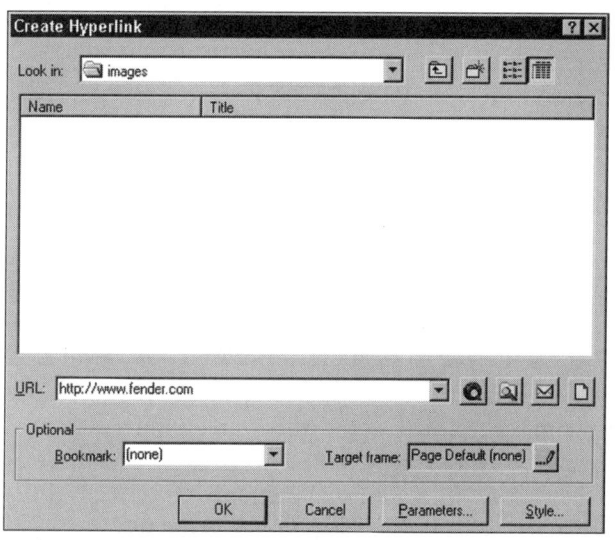

5. Click OK to close the Create Hyperlink dialog box. Your link shows up in FrontPage underlined and in blue. Figure 5-2 shows several hyperlinks that I have added.

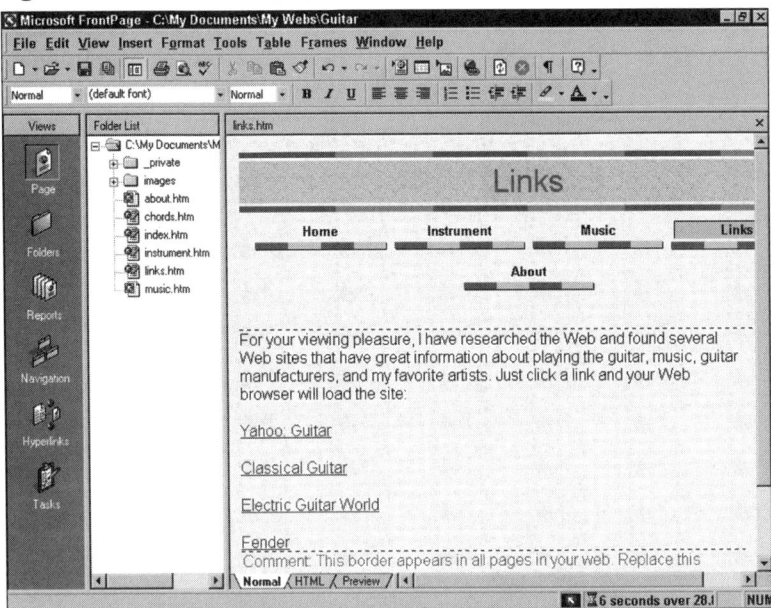

Chapter 5: Beefing Up Your Web Pages with Links, Lists, and Pictures 57

Figure 5-2: Links show up underlined and in blue.

Creating an e-mail link

E-mail links are a special type of hyperlink. Instead of using a Web address, e-mail links use an e-mail address. When a person clicks an e-mail link, his or her e-mail program opens and automatically addresses a message to the e-mail address of the e-mail hyperlink. This feature is great if you want to put your e-mail address on your Web site so that people can contact you. Follow these steps to create an e-mail link:

 1. Enter a name in your Web page to form the first part of the e-mail link. This can be your name or the name of another person you want to receive the e-mail. In the Guitar Web page, for example, I use the information in my lower shared border to create an e-mail link to myself.

2. Highlight the name you want to turn into an e-mail link with your mouse; then click the Hyperlink button on the toolbar. Doing so opens the Create Hyperlink dialog box.

3. Click the little envelope icon in the lower-right part of the dialog box. This icon tells FrontPage that you want to create an e-mail link. When you click it, the Create E-mail Hyperlink dialog box opens.

4. Enter the e-mail address of the person you want to receive the e-mail.

5. Click OK to close the Create E-mail Hyperlink dialog box. FrontPage automatically enters the correct address in the Create Hyperlink box. Click OK to close this dialog box. FrontPage updates your Web page, and you can see the e-mail link, shown in Figure 5-3, at the bottom of the Web page.

Figure 5-3: E-mail links look just like links to Web pages.

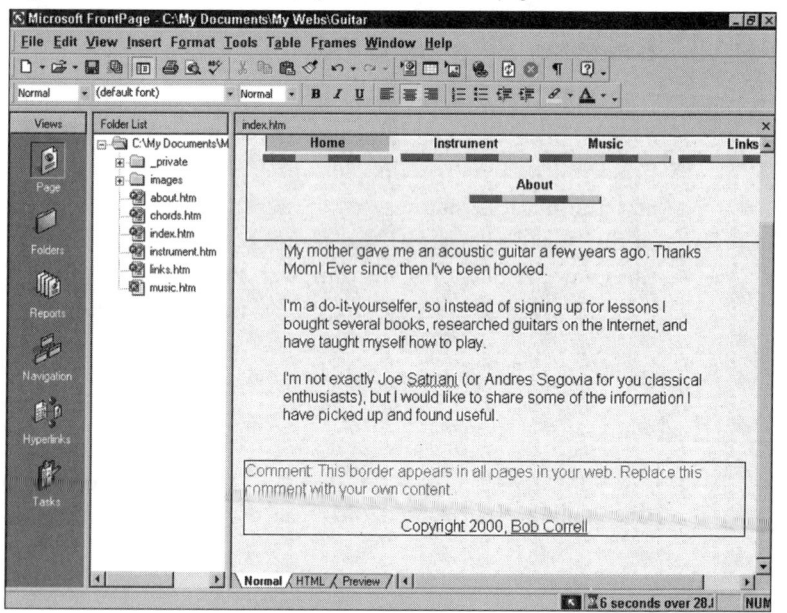

Putting Your Information into Lists

You can organize information on your Web page by creating lists. Lists help break information into manageable and understandable chunks for easy reading. You see them not only in Web pages but also in virtually all types of media, from magazines to books such as this one. Lists come in two main types: unordered (which may be bulleted) and ordered (or numbered). Bulleted lists have small bullets beside each item in the list, whereas each item in a numbered list has a number beside it, representing the order of importance of an item or a chronologically ordered process.

Tip

If you've ever created bulleted and numbered lists using Microsoft Word, you already know how to create them in FrontPage. Luckily for you, FrontPage uses the same tools as Word to create bulleted and numbered lists.

Creating bulleted lists

If you don't need your information to be displayed in a numerical order, create a bulleted list. You can still order your information, but each list item will have a bullet next to it. Follow these steps to create a bulleted list:

1. Start a new paragraph in your Web page by pressing Enter.

2. Click the Bulleted List icon on the toolbar. Doing so creates a bullet beside the line you are on.

3. Enter your first bullet and then press Enter to start a new line.

4. Keep typing bullets and pressing Enter until you finish your list.

> **Tip:** If you want to continue typing normal text after your last bulleted item, click the Bullets icon in the FrontPage toolbar to turn bullets off.

> **Tip:** Remember choosing a template for your Web back in Chapter 4? One option was to use Active Graphics. One neat feature of choosing Active Graphics is animated bullet icons (should the theme you have chosen support them).

Creating numbered lists

Use numbered lists if you want to create a list that has a definite order to it. Numbered steps are a good example. Each list item will have a number next to it. Follow these steps to create a numbered list:

1. Start a new paragraph in your Web page by pressing Enter.
2. Click the Numbered List icon on the toolbar. Doing so creates a number beside the line you are on.
3. Enter your first numbered item and then press Enter to start a new line.
4. Keep typing steps and pressing Enter until you finish your list.

> **Tip:** You can nest lists within one another, even if they are bulleted and numbered. For example, I could create a "top-level" list with the three types of guitars, and then "nest" lists with specific information about the particular type of guitar underneath each list item in the top-level list.

Adding Clip Art and Pictures to Your Page

Text, even if it is well formatted and contains interesting material, doesn't always tell the whole story. You can make your site much more compelling if you use colorful pictures. If you are working with logos or more visual information (such as guitar chords, which are hard to describe using text alone), you may even find that pictures are the best method of getting your message across to your audience.

Pictures can add a lot of pizzazz to your Web pages, but be careful. Always try to minimize the total file size of your graphics. When a person visits your Web site, their Web browser must download each graphic that you put in your Web pages before they can see them in their Web browser. And having numerous graphics can make a site take longer to download than most people are willing to wait.

Take a peek at the status bar of the FrontPage window to tell how long a page will take to download. FrontPage calculates how long it will take a person to load the page with a 28.8 Kbps modem and displays the time. A good rule is to ask yourself, "Would I wait this long?" If not, you should take some pictures out to try to reduce the overall size of your Web page.

Using clip art in your Web page

FrontPage comes with an extensive clip art library that you can use to add all kinds of pictures to your Web page. Because the pictures are already created for you, you don't have to worry about creating them yourself. This can save you a lot of time. Follow these steps to add clip art to your Web page:

  1. Open a Web page in the Page view and place your cursor where you want to insert the clip art.

  2. Select the Insert⇨Picture⇨Clip Art menu. Doing so opens the Clip Art Gallery.

  3. Browse the Clip Art categories or search for pictures (or Motion Clips, special animated graphics) that suit your purpose.

4. Select the picture and click the Insert Clip icon that appears, as shown in Figure 5-4.

Figure 5-4: After I searched for *guitar,* I found a suitable picture and am ready to insert it.

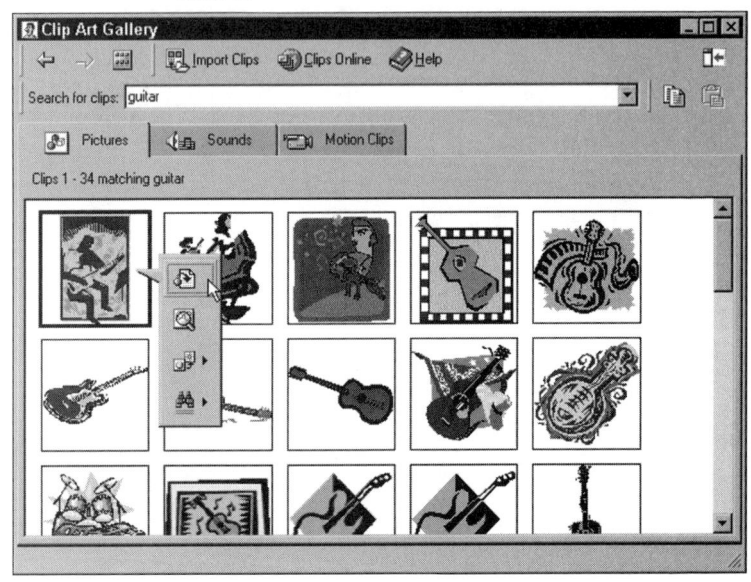

The picture will appear in your Web page at full size. If you want to resize it, select one of the small black boxes (called *handles*) that surround the picture and drag it to make the picture smaller. Figure 5-5 shows the clip art that I added to my home page. I made the picture smaller and aligned it on the left side of the page with the text wrapping to the right of the picture.

Chapter 5: Beefing Up Your Web Pages with Links, Lists, and Pictures   63

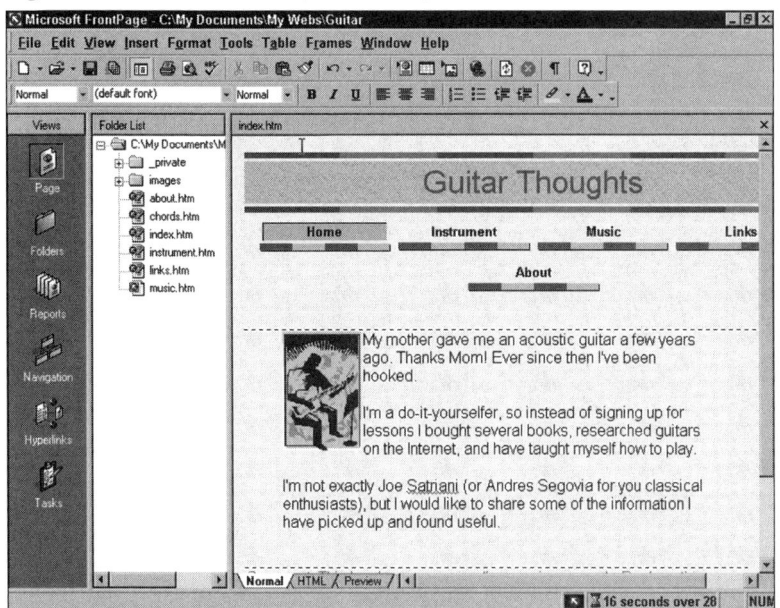

Figure 5-5: I've resized the picture and aligned the text around it.

Adding pictures to your Web page

The other route to adding pictures to your Web page is to gather or create them yourself. You can purchase CDs full of stock photography and other pictures, scan your own photos into your computer if you have a scanner, or create them in an image-editing program, such as Microsoft PhotoDraw or Image Composer.

> **Warning**
>
> Many pictures you will find on the Web are copyrighted. You may find yourself in legal trouble if you use them on your Web site without obtaining permission from their owner. Take special care to read any copyright information and abide by all applicable copyright laws.

Follow these steps to add your own pictures to your Web page:

1. Open a Web page in the Page view and place your cursor where you want to insert your picture.

2. Select the Insert➪Picture➪From File menu. Doing so opens the Picture dialog box.

3. Click the small Windows Explorer icon in the lower-right portion of the dialog box to browse for your picture file on your computer.

4. When you find the right picture, select it and click OK.

The Picture dialog box closes and your picture appears on your Web page. If necessary, you can resize the image as described previously.

The final result is shown in Figure 5-6.

Figure 5-6: I created this picture myself; the annotations are a part of the picture, not the Web page text.

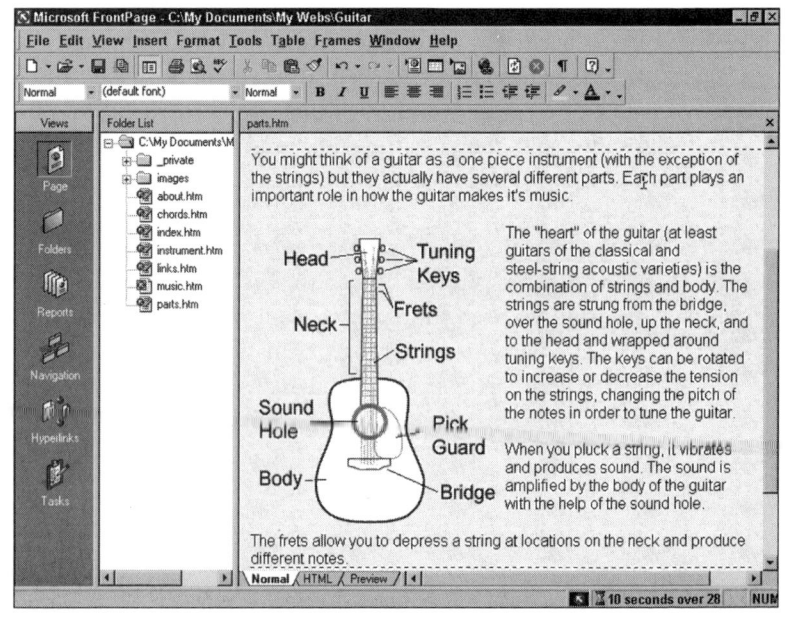

When you save Web pages to which you have added pictures, FrontPage asks whether saving the pictures in its Images directory is okay. Select Yes. This is important because you want to keep all your files together in your Web site directory. When you save your Web to a server, you won't get confused about what to include and thus possibly leave important files out.

CHAPTER 6
CREATING TABLES

IN THIS CHAPTER

- Creating tables in your Web pages
- Adding your own material inside tables
- Aligning the information inside a table
- Changing your table's width
- Adding or removing table rows or columns

Tables are a great way to organize information on your Web pages. To help you visualize what tables are and how they can be used, imagine a school classroom with a bunch of desks arranged in orderly rows and columns. You'll find a desk at the intersection of each row and column. Its job is to hold things. Each desk, for example, can hold a person's books, pens, pencils, and paper. No matter how many rows, columns, and desks there are in our classroom, they all behave exactly the same. A table in a Web page works a lot like this. It has a number of rows and columns that you decide on, and at the intersection of each row and column is a container, much like a desk, called a *cell*. Rather than put school supplies in your table cells, you put in bits of information.

They key is to find the right type of information to put in your cells. No benefit exists, for example, from putting a paragraph of text such as this one in a table. Organizing the notes on a guitar fretboard into a table, however, can be truly helpful. Take a look at Table 6-1 to see how I can organize this information in a table.

Table 6-1: Whole Notes on a Guitar by Fret Number

0	1	2	3	4	5	6	7	8	9	10	11	12
E	F		G		A		B	C		D		E
B	C		D		E	F		G		A		B
G		A		B	C		D		E		F	G
D		E	F		G		A		B	C		D
A		B	C		D		E	F		G		A
E	F		G		A		B	C		D		E

In this chapter, I show you how to create tables in your Web pages and put information inside them, such as what you see in Table 6-1.

Creating a Table

Although FrontPage offers several ways to create tables, the easiest one is to use the Insert Table button on the toolbar. There's a trick to it, though, so watch carefully. Follow these steps to create a table:

1. Run FrontPage, open your Web, and open a Web page in the Page view. You put your table in this page. (In this example, I add Table 6-1, shown previously, a new Web page in my guitar site.)

2. Place your cursor where you want to insert your table. If your Web page is empty, you must put your table at the top of the page.

3. Click the Insert Table button from the toolbar and hold your mouse button down. Notice that Figure 6-1 shows a grid that opens just below the button. This grid represents the number of rows and columns you can add to your table.

4. Drag your mouse down and to the right to highlight the number of rows and columns you want to add, as shown in Figure 6-2. If you run up against the edge of the grid, the grid will expand and let you add more rows and columns than it originally displayed. Notice that, in the lower part of the grid, FrontPage informs you how many rows and columns you have selected. If you count the number of rows and columns in Table 6-1, shown previously, you can see that I need to create a table that is 7 rows by 13 columns.

Figure 6-1: The Insert Table button allows you to select the number of rows and columns for your table.

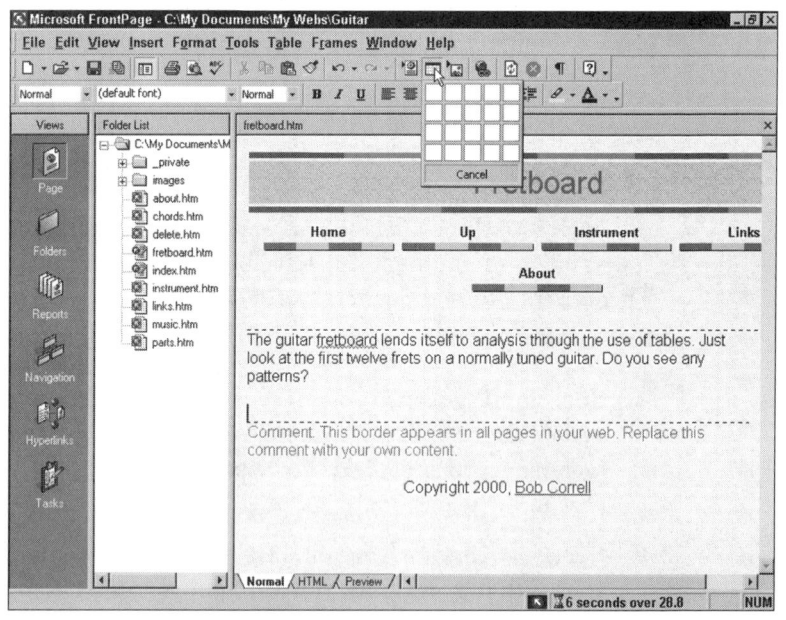

5. When you are happy with the size of your table, release your mouse button. FrontPage creates a table in your Web page with the dimensions you've chosen, as shown in Figure 6-3. By default, the table should take up the entire width of your Web page. You can check this by selecting the Table ➪ Properties ➪ Table menu and looking to see that the Specify Width option is checked and reads 100 percent.

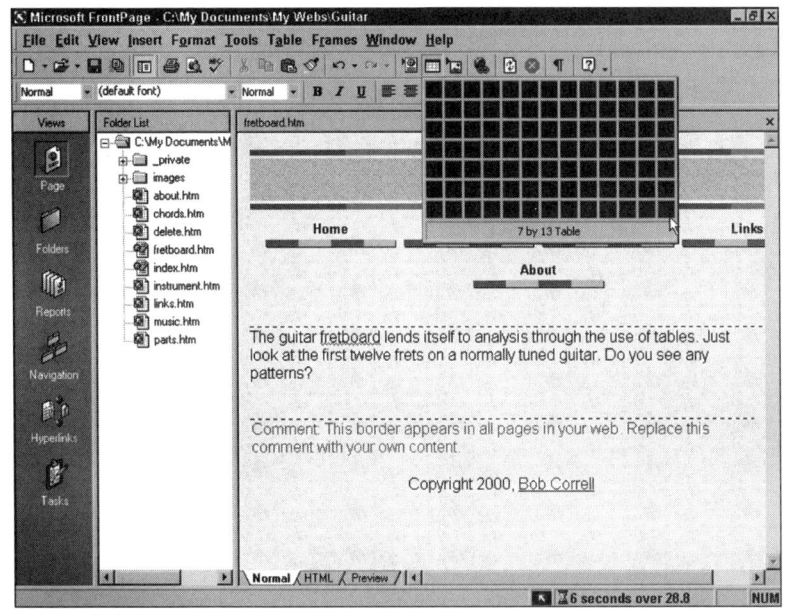

Figure 6-2: Keep dragging your mouse to make your table larger.

Take a look at your new table for a minute. Notice that the table takes up the entire width of your Web page. I show you how to make it smaller later in the chapter. The table also has borders around all the rows, columns, and cells. These help divide the table so that people can easily tell what's in one cell versus another. You can turn these borders off (I explain how later). In addition, the table is empty. You'll have to add your own content to it. Before going on, take a few minutes to play around and create some tables on your own. Try making tables with different numbers of rows and columns.

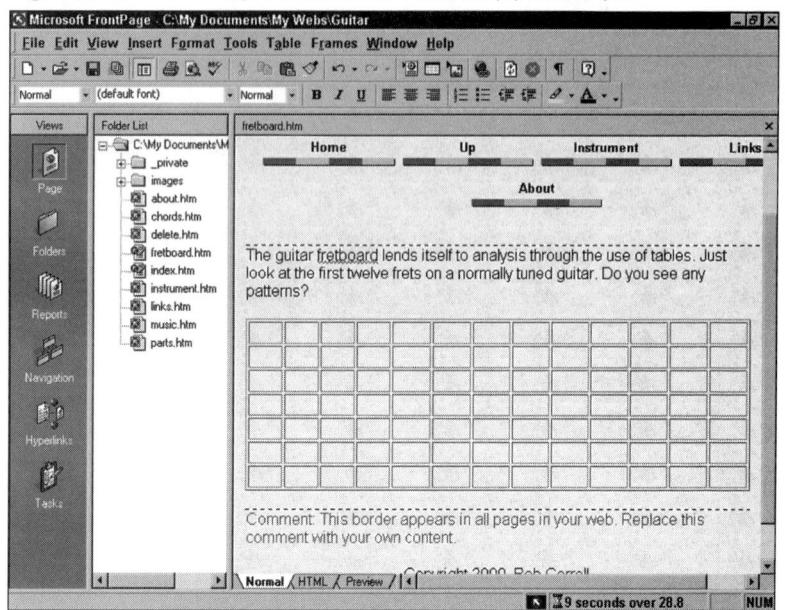

Figure 6-3: FrontPage creates a nice, new, but empty table for you.

Working with Table Content

Empty tables are obviously not what you're after, so go ahead and put something into the one you just created. After that, you can work on aligning the contents of your cells.

Adding material to a table

Okay, you have an empty table sitting there on your Web page that needs something in it. Simply click inside a cell to position your cursor; then start typing. The trick is remembering that each cell is an independent entity. If you press Enter, you'll start a new line, but it will be inside the same cell that you started in. Press Tab to move from one cell to the next, click your mouse inside any cell you want to work on, or use your arrow keys to move around between cells just as you would in a spreadsheet program, such as Microsoft

Excel. Figure 6-4 shows that I've successfully added my guitar information to my new table.

Figure 6-4: Click in each cell and then add text or other objects.

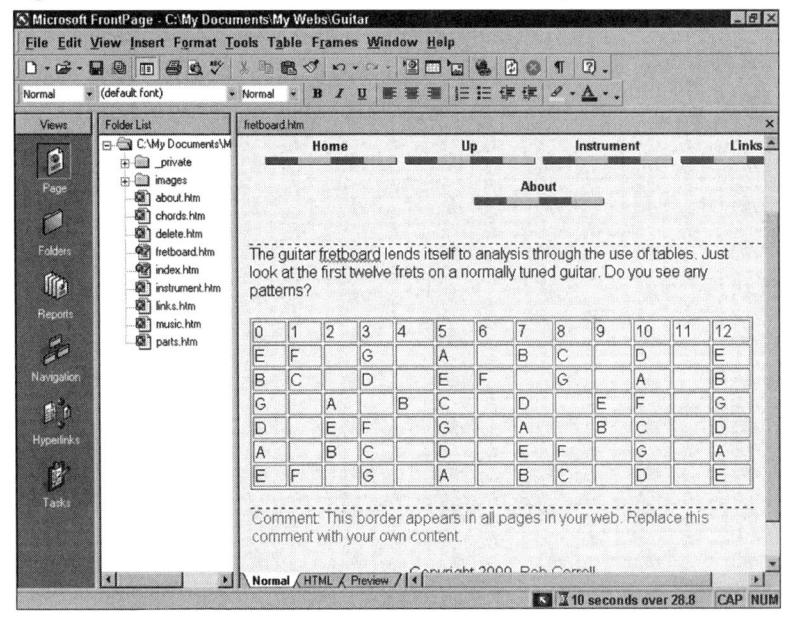

It looks sort of plain at the moment, but you can format the text inside a table just as you would do in a normal paragraph. Use bold, underlining, different fonts, text colors, and other tricks from the Formatting toolbar at the top of the FrontPage screen to make things stand out. (For more on the Formatting toolbar, see Chapter 3.) Notice also that the text is aligned to the left.

Aligning items in your table cells

Use the alignment buttons on the Formatting toolbar if you want to change the alignment of your table cells. Simply place your cursor in the cell you want to change, and then click whatever alignment button you wish (Left, Center, or Right).

If you want to change the alignment for more than one cell at a time, follow these guidelines:

- **Rows:** Select an entire row by placing your cursor in a cell on that row; then select the Table➪Select➪Row menu item. Doing so highlights the row. You can then click an alignment button and apply the alignment you choose to the entire selected row.

- **Columns:** Follow the same steps as you do for rows, but select the Table➪Select➪Column menu item instead.

- **Groups of cells:** Highlight the cells you want to change with your mouse. Click in the top-left cell and hold your mouse button down; then drag your mouse to the lower right until you've highlighted the cells you want. Release your mouse button. Next, select the appropriate alignment button.

- **The entire table:** Highlight the table just as you do a group of cells, but start in the very top-left cell and highlight the entire table. Then select an alignment button.

> **Tip:** You can use these selection techniques for more than just changing alignment. For example, you can select the contents of several cells and delete them in one fell swoop by pressing Delete. You can also change the formatting of the text in several cells. For example, you could make the top row of your table stand out as a heading by selecting the top row and bolding the contents of the entire row in one fell swoop.

Working with the Table Itself

Now that you have the hang of creating tables and adding content, you're ready to move on to changing the properties of the table. Some of these tasks, such as aligning your table or using different colors, are cosmetic in nature. In other words, they simply make the table look the way you want it.

Others, such as changing the table's width and adding or removing rows and columns, change more fundamental properties of the table.

Changing the width of your table

You probably won't want all of your tables to take up the entire width of a Web page. You may want a table to always be 50 percent of the width of the Web page, for example, or define a table more precisely to be an exact number of pixels wide. There are pros and cons to each approach. The "proportional" (using percentages) approach is great when you want your table to take up a certain amount of space regardless of the size of a person's Web browser window. Whether a visitor has his Web browser maximized to take up the entire screen or reduced so that it occupies only a small portion of the monitor screen, your table will always be (as a percentage of the Web page) the same width. The pixel approach is best when you need exact control over the width of your table and aren't concerned about a visitor needing to resize his browser to see all the information.

To set the width of your table using either approach, do the following:

1. Open a Web page that has a table that you want to change in the Page view and place your cursor inside your table.

2. Select the Table⇨Properties⇨Table menu. Doing so opens the Table Properties dialog box, shown in Figure 6-5.

3. To enter the width of your table as a percentage of your total Web page width, click the In Percent option in the upper-left corner of the dialog box and enter the percent number in the text field. (The initial value is always 100%.) To enter the width of your table in numbers of pixels, select the In Pixels option and enter the number of pixels in the text field.

4. Click OK to close the dialog box and return to the Page view. FrontPage automatically resizes your table.

> If you have content that requires more space than you have set, such as a picture that is very wide, the table will expand on its own to display it.

Figure 6-5: Change the width of your table to a percentage of the total Web page.

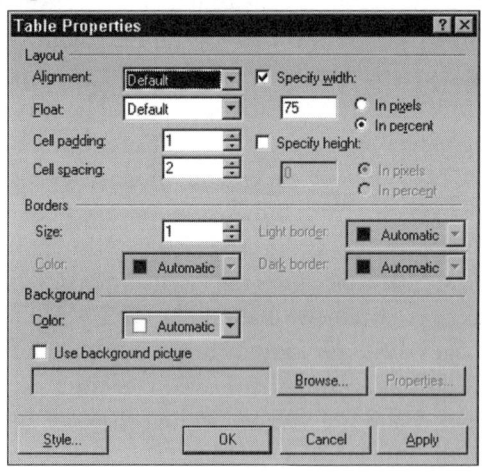

Aligning your table on your Web page

If you have changed the width of your table to less than 100 percent of the total page width, you can align the table to the left, right, or center of your Web page just as you align a paragraph of text. First, place your cursor in the table. Then select the Table⇨Select⇨Table menu and choose an alignment from the Alignment pull-down menu.

Adding and removing rows and columns

If you find, after you've created your table, that you have either not enough rows or columns or too many, you easily fix the situation. Follow these guidelines to add or remove rows and columns:

- **Adding:** Place your cursor in your table where you want to add your row or column; then select the Table➪Insert➪Rows or Columns menu. Doing so opens the Add Rows or Columns dialog box. Select the Rows or Columns options, depending on what you want to add, and then enter the number of rows or columns you want to add. Finally, choose whether you want to insert your new rows or columns before or after the current location of your cursor.

- **Deleting:** Place your cursor in the row or column you want to delete and then select the Table➪Select➪Row or the Table➪Select➪Column menu, depending on what you want to delete. Doing so highlights the row or column you plan to delete. After it is highlighted, select the Table➪Delete Cells menu. Poof! It's gone.

Working with borders

Web browsers draw borders around your table and divide up all your rows and columns. Sometimes this division is exactly what you want. You may even want bigger borders to create a frame around your table. In some situations, however, borders actually detract from the appearance of your table. If you feel this is the case, you'll want to remove your table's borders.

In all cases, place your mouse cursor inside a table and select the Table➪Properties➪Table menu. Doing so opens the same Table Properties dialog box shown previously in Figure 6-5.

In the middle of the dialog box is an area called Borders. Enter the size of the border you want in the Size field or use the arrow buttons beside it to increase or decrease the border size.

CliffsNotes Creating Your First Web Site with FrontPage 2000

Figure 6-6 shows two versions of one table: The top table has no borders, and the bottom table has a border of 5 (which is the number of screen pixels the border occupies). Notice that I'm previewing the Web page with the Preview tab. Experiment with borders to see what you like; you can always go back and change what you've done!

Figure 6-6: The top table has no border and the bottom table has a border of 5.

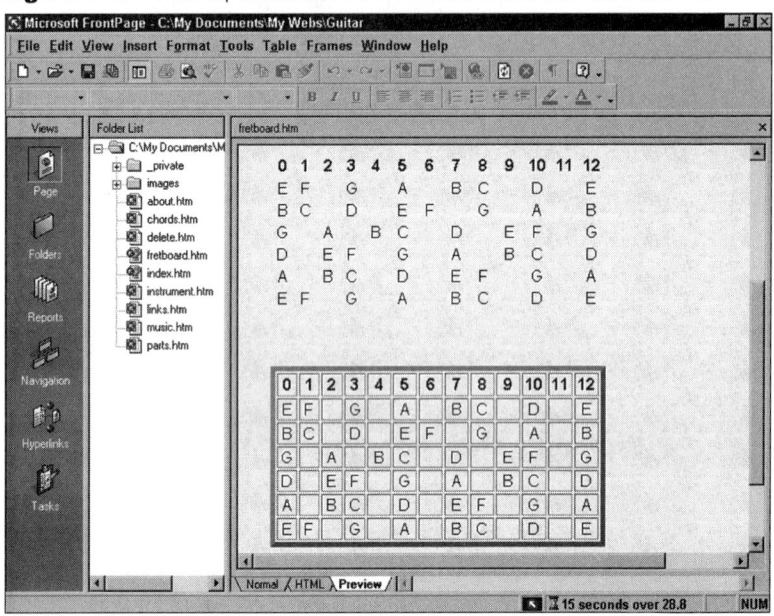

CHAPTER 7
ADDING EXTRAS: MULTIMEDIA, DYNAMIC HTML, AND MORE

IN THIS CHAPTER

- Choosing a target Web browser
- Adding multimedia — inline sound and video
- Using Dynamic HTML in your Web pages
- Adding other extras

If you're bored with text-only Web pages, or pictures that just sit there, you've come to the right chapter. FrontPage allows you to add many special effects that range from background sounds to video to hopping, skipping, and jumping graphics and text. (All the hopping, skipping, and jumping is made possible by *Dynamic HTML,* a souped-up version of the standard HTML, or Hypertext Markup Language, used to create Web pages.)

Although adding special effects to your Web pages can be fun and rewarding, there are challenges to overcome. You should always consider your target audience and what type of Web browser they might use. Not all Web browsers are created equal. Just as a person needs a Pentium III computer with loads of RAM rather than an ancient 486/33 to run the most current and technologically demanding software, if you create a Web page with advanced Web technologies, only certain Web browsers will be able to properly view those pages. You simply have to choose what audience you want to cater to and stick with the appropriate effects.

In this chapter, I show you how to add some "chrome" to your Web pages. These effects are not always compatible across the different types of Web browsers, but you can choose a target Web browser and FrontPage will make sure that all your pages can be viewed by that set of browsers. Some effects, such as adding horizontal lines, are compatible across all Web browsers.

Setting a Target Web Browser

Before you decide what extras to include in your Web pages, you need to determine a Web browser, or set of browsers, that you plan to target. In Table 7-1, I summarize how different Web browsers, Microsoft Internet Explorer (MSIE), and Netscape Navigator (NNav), support a few of the effects used by FrontPage. Don't worry if some of the terms appear unfamiliar; you'll get acquainted with them over the course of the chapter. Although you may not want to use all these effects, this table gives you a good idea of the differences between these popular Web browsers.

Table 7-1: Comparing Effects across Web Browsers

Effect	MSIE 3	MSIE 4+	NNav 3	NNav 4+
Background sounds	Yes	Yes	No	No
Inline sounds	Yes	Yes	Yes	Yes
Dynamic HTML (limitations)	No	Yes	No	Yes
Hover buttons	Yes	Yes	Yes	Yes
Marquees	Yes	Yes	No	No
Symbols	Yes	Yes	Yes	Yes
Horizontal lines	Yes	Yes	Yes	Yes

If you are interested in reaching the widest possible audience, you will have to eschew using more advanced effects such as Dynamic HTML. If your site is more oriented toward the cutting edge and you think your audience has access to the latest Web browsers, then by all means go ahead and use whatever technologies you can to achieve your effects. Follow these steps to target a Web browser:

1. Run FrontPage and open your Web site.

2. Select the Tools⇨Page Options menu. Doing so opens the Page Options dialog box, as shown in Figure 7-1, which allows you to set several options for your Web pages.

3. Select the Compatibility tab, as shown in Figure 7-1. This tab lets you set the target Web browser for your Web pages.

4. Select a browser (or set of browsers) from the pull-down Browsers menu as well as a version (3+, 4+, or custom) for the browser(s) that you wish to support. Notice in the figure that some of the individual technologies at the bottom of the dialog box become unchecked or grayed out. This tells you that FrontPage won't use these technologies.

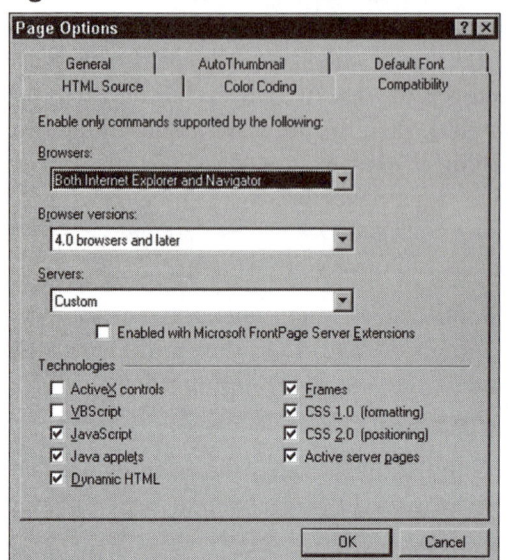

Figure 7-1: Select a Web browser and a browser version to target your Web pages.

5. Click OK to close the dialog box. From this point forward, FrontPage will use only the technologies that were checked in the Page Options dialog box as you create your Web pages.

Adding Sounds and Video

Sound and video can add a lot to your Web pages if you use them wisely. Remember, the Web browser of a person visiting your Web site has to download sound and video files to play them. Because these files can be enormous (and thus take a long time to download for some in your prospective audience), choose wisely.

Adding background sound

You can use background sounds to set a mood for your Web pages. Background sounds play in the background after a

Web page loads into a person's browser. With the guitar Web site, for example, I might want play a short passage of guitar music to add ambiance. One note of caution however. Background sounds are not compatible in all Web browsers. If you have your Web pages set to be compatible with Web browsers other than Internet Explorer, you won't be able to include background sounds. Follow these steps to add a background sound:

1. Open a Web page in the Page view.

2. Select File➪Properties. Doing so opens the Page Properties dialog box, as shown in Figure 7-2.

3. In the Background Sound part of the dialog box, enter the location of the file containing your background sound as well as its filename, or choose Browse if you need help finding it. You can choose any one of several different types of sound files for your background sounds. Three types — .wav, .midi, and .au files — are most commonly used on the Web.

4. If you want your background sound to play over and over again, make sure that the Loop Forever box remains checked. Otherwise, uncheck Loop Forever and enter the number of times you want the sound to loop.

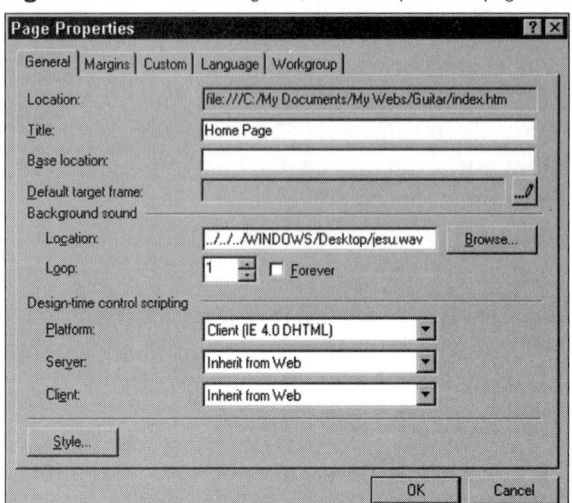

Figure 7-2: Add background sounds to your Web pages to create a unique mood.

5. Click OK to close the dialog box.

When you save your Web page, FrontPage asks whether you also want to save your background sound file within the folder structure underneath your Web folder on your hard drive. Whenever you add graphics or sounds to your Web site, FrontPage will always ask to save the files within this Web folder structure. When you allow it to do so, all of your Web's files are kept together in a nice, organized location so you don't forget them when you publish your Web to the Internet.

Choose Change Folder and select the folder in your Web site where you want your sound to be saved. When you publish your Web site, the sound will be included. If you don't properly save your sound file to your Web site, it will not work when you save your site to a Web server. Click OK to close the dialog box. FrontPage saves your Web page and makes sure that the sound file is stored in the correct location in your Web site.

Adding inline sound

Background sounds are played in the background of your Web pages. A person visiting your Web site has no control over the background sound — it will download and play regardless of their wishes. If you want to add other sounds to your Web pages, sounds that they do have control over, add inline sound.

When you add inline sound, people's Web browser will display audio controls and allow them to start, stop, and replay the sound. I may want to include this type of sound in my guitar Web site so that people can listen to different guitar chords. Follow these steps to add inline sounds to your Web pages:

 1. Place your cursor in your Web page where you want to insert the inline sound and select the Insert➪Advanced➪Plug-In menu. This opens the Plug-In Properties dialog box, shown in Figure 7-3, which allows you to choose a sound file to place in your Web page.

 2. Choose Browse, find the sound file on your computer, and double-click it to select it. The sound file will show up in the Data Source text box in the Plug-In Properties dialog box, as shown in Figure 7-3.

 3. Enter an appropriate message in the Message for Browsers without Plug-In Support text field (something like "Sorry, you do not have the appropriate plug-in to hear this sound file"). Your message will automatically be displayed for people who use a browser that doesn't support inline sounds.

 4. Click OK to close the dialog box. A stylized graphic of a computer plug-in shows up on your Web page in Page view. This is a placeholder to remind you that you've inserted a plug-in at that location on your Web page. Select the Preview tab if you want to see (or hear) the actual plug-in in action.

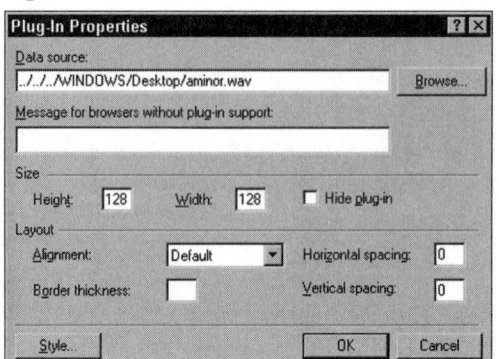

Figure 7-3: Add inline sounds for more individualized sound uses.

Adding video

Adding videos to your Web pages is as easy as adding sound, but compatibility issues may exist. The simplest way to include a video file is to select the Insert➪Picture➪Video menu. Doing so opens a Select File dialog box. All you need to do is find the video file (in the proper format, which is shown in the dialog box) and choose OK. The video appears in your Web page and plays when people open the page in their Web browser. The one drawback to this method is that it works only with Internet Explorer. If you have chosen both Web browsers (Internet Explorer and Netscape Navigator) as targets, the menu option to add videos is disabled.

The alternate, and most compatible, method for adding videos to your Web pages is to use the Insert➪Advanced➪Plug-In menu. When you select this menu, the Plug-In Properties dialog box opens. Locate your video file by using the Browse button. This action puts the filename and location in the Data Source field of the dialog box. You should add a message for people who may not be able to view the video in the Message field and then click OK. When the dialog box closes, you see a plug-in graphic in the Page view. If you want to see the video, select the Preview tab and, presto, your video appears!

Adding Dynamic HTML to Your Pages

With the introduction of Dynamic HTML, you can now add cutting-edge dynamic effects to your Web pages. Please note that Dynamic HTML works best with Internet Explorer. Although it can work with Netscape Navigator, your options are far more limited. *Events* and *effects* make dynamic effects possible. *Events* are triggered when something happens in a Web page, such as the page loading into a person's Web browser or when someone moves a mouse over something on your Web page. *Effects* are responses to an event. For example, you might have a heading that magically flies into your Web page when the page loads into a Web browser. It starts out completely off the Web page and comes in from any side. You can even have words spiral into your Web page or fly off your Web page when you click them!

Most events (clicking something, double-clicking, or moving your mouse over an object or text) are available only when you are targeting Internet Explorer. One event (when the Web page loads into the Web browser) is compatible with both Internet Explorer and Netscape Navigator. You should create a Web page and try all these effects, experimenting with them to find a few that you like best. Follow these steps to add dynamic effects to your Web page:

1. Open your Web site.
2. Open a Web page in the Page view.
3. Select some text or a picture and choose Format➪Dynamic HTML Effects.
4. Choose an event, such as mouse over or double-click.
5. Choose an effect to apply, such as fly out, formatting, or fly in.
6. Choose settings to apply to the effect.

7. When you are finished, you can close the DHTML Effects toolbar by clicking the X in the top-right corner of the toolbar.

The DHTML effect will be highlighted on your screen when you are in Page view to remind you that you're using a DHTML effect. Should you want to remove the effect, open the DHTML Effects toolbar, place your mouse cursor in the highlighted area, and then select Remove Effect from the DHTML Effects toolbar. Presto! It's gone.

Adding More Extras

The fun doesn't stop with sound, video, and Dynamic HTML. You can add a wide range of other effects with FrontPage. A complete list of additional doodads would be far too lengthy for this book, so I cover just a few of the fun ones here.

Using hover buttons

A hover button is a button that you can put in your Web pages that, when clicked, activates a hyperlink to another Web page or file. The neat thing about hover buttons is that they change color or shape when people move their mouse over them. Themes also include these effects on the Navigation buttons as long as you checked Active Graphics in the Themes dialog box. Follow these steps to insert a hover button in your Web page:

1. Select the Insert➪Component➪Hover Button menu. The Hover Button Properties dialog box appears, as shown in Figure 7-4.

2. Enter the text you want to display on the button.

3. Select a Web page to link to.

4. Change any other settings that you like, such as the color of the button or its size.

5. Choose an effect and effect color. The effects (color fill, color average, glow, reverse glow, light glow, bevel out, and bevel in) all produce different variations on a theme. Experiment with the effects to see which one you like best.

Figure 7-4: Use hover buttons to link to other files or Web pages.

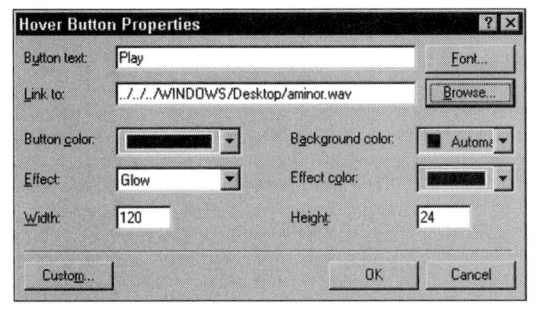

6. Click OK to finish and close the dialog box. You need to save your Web page after inserting hover buttons so that you can preview the button effects.

Adding a marquee

Use a marquee if you want to scroll text across the screen when a person is looking at one of your Web pages. Follow these steps to add a marquee to a Web page:

1. Choose the Insert⇨Component⇨Marquee menu.

2. In the Marquee Properties dialog box, enter the text you want to scroll across the screen, as shown in Figure 7-5.

3. Change the other settings to adjust the marquee to suit your goals, such as what direction the text scrolls or how many times you want it to repeat.

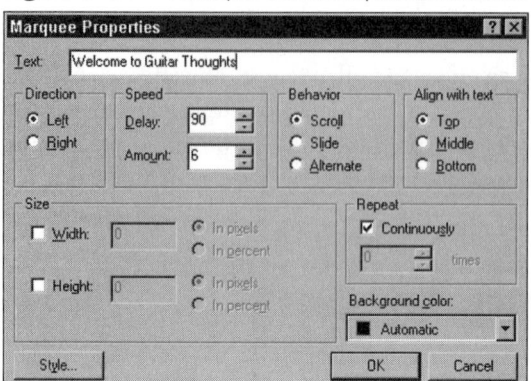

Figure 7-5: A marquee continuously scrolls text across the screen.

Inserting Symbols

If you need to insert a symbol, such as a copyright symbol, follow these steps:

1. Place your cursor in a Web page where you want to add a symbol and select the Insert⇨Symbols menu.
2. Select a symbol to insert, and then press Insert.
3. Select Close to close the dialog box.

Adding horizontal lines

You can use horizontal lines to visually break up your Web page into different sections. Choose Insert⇨Horizontal Line to add a horizontal line on your Web page at the location of your cursor. Figure 7-6 shows a horizontal line that I've inserted to create a break across my Web page.

After you have inserted your horizontal line, you can change its properties by double-clicking it. You can choose a different width, height, horizontal alignment, color, and shading. Go ahead and experiment with different types of horizontal lines until you find something that you really like!

Chapter 7: Adding Extras: Multimedia, Dynamic HTML, and More 89

Figure 7-6: Horizontal lines break your Web pages into distinct areas.

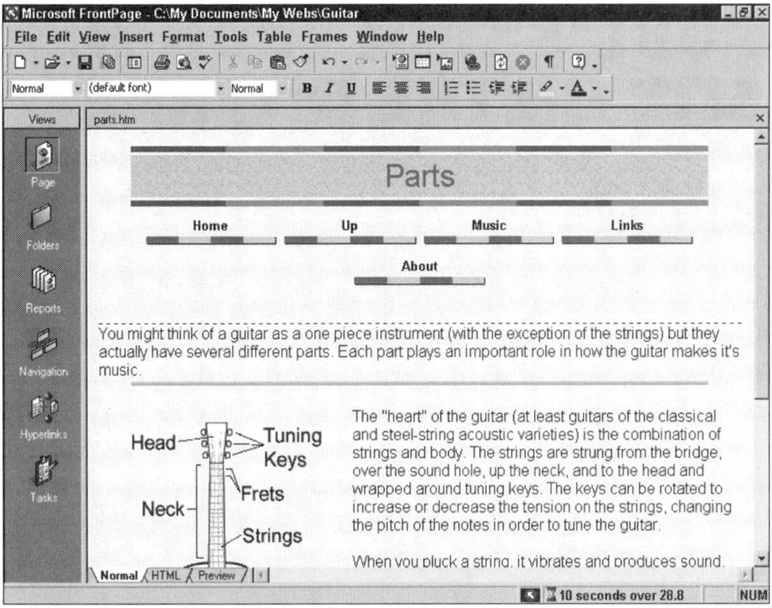

CHAPTER 8
PUBLISHING YOUR WEB SITE ON THE INTERNET

IN THIS CHAPTER

- Making sure that your Web site and computer are ready
- Finding a Web server to host your Web site
- Publishing your Web site on the Internet

Publishing your Web site on the Internet isn't like publishing a book or magazine. Thankfully, you don't need an expensive printing press, reams of paper, and gallons of ink. You do need several things, however:

- Your computer, with the necessary hardware, such as a modem, to connect to the Internet
- A dial-up Internet connection so that you can get online
- FrontPage so that you can create your Web site
- Your Web site, which you will publish online
- Space on a Web server to store your Web site

In this chapter, I show you how to gather all these pieces together and get them working for you to publish your Web site on the Internet. After you publish your site, anyone with an Internet connection and a Web browser will be able to see your Web site online — provided that you give them the Web address!

Getting Things Ready

Because publishing your Web site on the Internet involves going online, it's important that you set up your computer to be able to dial your Internet Service Provider (ISP) and connect to the Internet.

Preparing your computer

You need to have two very important hardware-related items ready to publish your Web site on the Internet: your computer and a modem. Modems come in two flavors: internal and external. It doesn't really matter which one you have — it's largely a matter of personal taste. I prefer external modems because they have status lights that blink on and off to tell me what the modem is doing and whether it is transmitting or receiving. External modems also have a convenient power switch so that you can turn them on and off. Having a power switch lets you reset your modem without having to reboot your computer.

You should have your modem installed and configured before you try to publish your Web site. Unless you are comfortable with opening your computer case, you should have a trained professional install an internal modem. External modems are easier. All you need to do is plug the modem into a power source, plug your telephone line into the phone line connector on the back of your modem, and plug your modem into the correct connection in the back of your computer. Restart your computer so that Windows can detect your new hardware, and then follow any instructions that pop up on your screen. If you need to install the modem drivers (the software that allows the modem to operate in Windows) yourself, you should refer to your modem's manual.

You also need a dial-up Internet account. You can't save your Web site to floppy disks and mail it to your Internet Service Provider (ISP)! You've got to go online, connect to your ISP, and then use FrontPage to upload your Web site to the server's hard drive.

You should refer to the documentation your ISP sent you to set up your Internet connection. You may either have to run a setup program provided by your ISP or configure a dial-up connection manually. Either way, a dial-up connection allows you to click an icon that tells your modem to dial your ISP and connect to the Internet.

Your Web site

Next, you need to make sure that all your Web pages have the right information in them and look the way you want them to. You also need to verify that all your hyperlinks and navigation buttons work. Before you publish your Web on the Internet, take the time to go through your Web site — page by page — in the FrontPage Preview window and in a real Web browser.

Open your Home Page in the Page view and select the Preview tab to look your Web site over inside FrontPage. Open your Web and then choose File➪Preview in Browser if you want to see how your Web looks in your Web browser. I'm testing my guitar Web site in Microsoft Internet Explorer, as shown in Figure 8-1.

Go ahead and connect to the Internet as you're testing your Web site. This way, you can click any hyperlinks you have that connect to external sites and see whether the addresses are correct and the sites still exist.

Figure 8-1: Test your Web site in your Web browser before you publish it online.

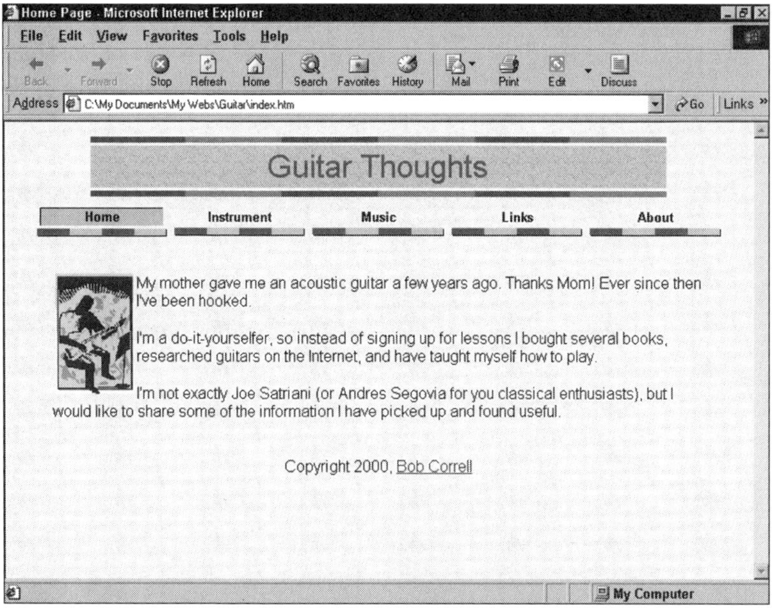

Finding a Server

Your Web site needs to be saved to a Web server so that people on the Internet can see it. Web servers are computers that are permanently connected to the Internet and run special software that allows people to view Web pages stored on that computer with Web browsers.

Using your Internet Service Provider's server

If you already have a dial-up Internet account with an ISP, visit its Web page and see what its Web hosting services are. Researching your ISP's Web hosting services is probably the easiest and cheapest way for you to find an online home for your Web. Most ISPs offer free Web hosting services but may restrict the total size of your Web to a few megabytes of space.

They may also tell you that if your Web site generates too much monthly traffic, you may be charged more. Normally these restrictions aren't a problem. Most personal Web sites aren't that large and don't attract millions of visits, or *hits*, per month.

Finding a Registered Web Presence Provider

You can also search Microsoft's Web site for a Registered Web Presence Provider. Such a company offers services that take advantage of some of the capabilities unique to Webs created with FrontPage 2000, such as hit counters (which tally the number of hits your site receives). Registered Web Presence Providers have special software, called FrontPage Server Extensions, installed on their server, allowing them to do perform these special services. Microsoft has a Web page, shown in Figure 8-2, especially set up so that you can search for Web Presence Providers or see whether your ISP is one.

Tip: Some companies charge extra if you want to be able to use FrontPage Server Extensions. If you're on a budget, forgo this and stick with a "clean" Web site — one that doesn't require a server running FrontPage Server Extensions. You'll miss out on some of the unique FrontPage Web site features, but chances are no one will notice but you.

Figure 8-2: Microsoft has a Web site that lets you search for Web Presence Providers.

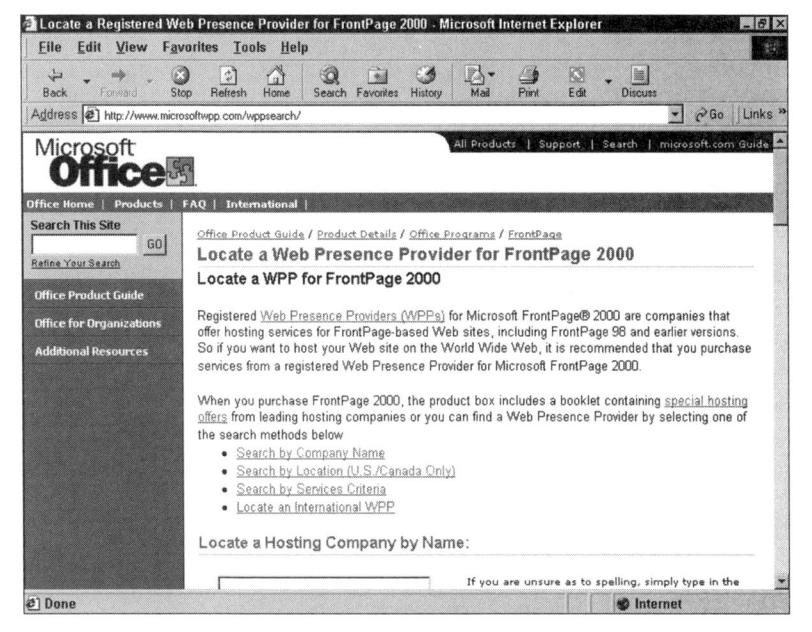

Determining Your Web Address

An important part of publishing your Web site is getting your Web address from the company hosting your site. Your Web address is what will allow you, and the people you tell about your site, to open it in a Web browser. Web addresses are all unique, and normally take the form of www.somesite.com. If your ISP hosts your site, your address will probably be a combination of its main Web page address and your user name. For example, if my username at www.somesite.com is correll, my Web address would probably be www.somesite.com/~correll. Make sure to check with your Web site host to get your exact address correct. You don't want to make any mistakes!

> **Tip:** If you want a more personalized Web address, based on your name or some other slogan you like (like www.guitarthoughts.com, which would be a good one for my example), you can ask your Web host about getting a domain name for your Web site. This will cost some extra money, because there is a yearly fee to register domain names on the Internet.

Publishing Your Web Site

You're finally here: ready to publish your Web site. If you want other people to be able to visit your Web site, you must save it to a Web server on the Internet. Otherwise, all that time and effort you spent creating your dream Web site will be wasted. Follow these steps to publish your Web site on the Internet:

1. Connect to your ISP and get online.

2. Launch FrontPage and open the Web site you want to publish on the Internet.

3. Select the File➪Publish Web menu. Doing so opens the Publish Web dialog box, as shown in Figure 8-3.

4. Enter the address you received from your ISP or Web hosting company in the location field.

Figure 8-3: Your ISP should provide the address you enter in this dialog box.

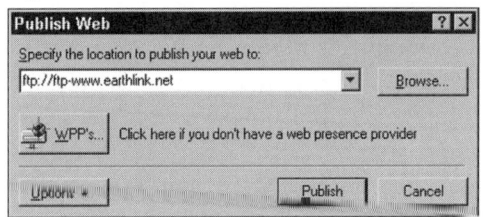

Chapter 8: Publishing Your Web Site on the Internet

5. Press Publish, and FrontPage connects to your ISP or Web hosting company using your default dial-up Internet account. You may need to enter a username and password before the Web server lets you begin publishing. This information will be provided to you by your ISP and normally is the username and password you use to connect in the first place. After successfully entering your username and password, you see a progress dialog box as FrontPage begins to send your Web site over the Internet to be stored on your Web server. When FrontPage finishes this task, it displays a dialog box telling you it has been successfully completed.

6. The last step is to make sure that the Web site you just published works. Launch your Web browser, enter the Web address into the address field, and press Enter to connect to your Web site. If all goes well, you see your Web site open in your browser. Test your site while you are online to make sure that everything works properly.

If you are publishing your Web site for the first time, you don't need to worry about the Options button shown in Figure 8-3. After you've published your Web site, you'll probably make changes over time. If not, you should really consider doing so! A static Web site is boring and people won't return after they find that you aren't updating it.

When you begin to make changes, you need to republish your Web. After all, your new Web pages won't do anyone any good if all they do is sit on your hard drive. FrontPage has a neat feature to help save you time when you republish your Web. Follow the same steps that you did to initially publish your Web, but before you select the Publish button, click the Options button and see what's inside. FrontPage will expand the Publish Web dialog box, as shown in Figure 8-4, and give you the option of transmitting only the pages that have changed or republishing your entire Web site. If you have a large Web site and only a few pages have been changed, choosing the Publish Changed Pages Only option will really save you time.

Figure 8-4:   Choose the Options button to publish only the pages that have changed.

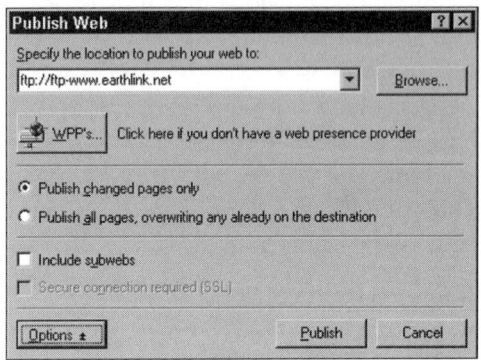

CHAPTER 9
MAINTAINING AND UPDATING YOUR WEB SITE

IN THIS CHAPTER

- Checking your pages and site for spelling errors
- Using the Site Summary report to maintain your site
- Verifying and fixing broken hyperlinks
- Continually updating your site

After you publish your new Web site on the Internet, you need to maintain and update it regularly. It's like having a pet. If you feed it regularly and give it some tender loving care, it will flourish. If you neglect it, however, your Web site may eventually fall into disrepair and people will stop visiting it. Not many people want to visit the same site over and over again!

In this chapter, I show you a few techniques for keeping your Web site in tip-top shape. I show you how to check your Web pages for spelling errors, verify all the hyperlinks in your Web, and update your Web site.

Maintaining Your Web Site

Not many people enjoy maintaining their Web site as much as they did creating it in the first place, but it's a chore you have to do to keep your Web site running smoothly. You should regularly check for spelling errors and run through several FrontPage reports to make sure that your site is healthy.

Spell-checking individual Web pages

Checking for spelling errors in FrontPage is very much like spell-checking in Microsoft Word. Follow these steps to check for errors in your Web pages:

1. Open your Web site and then open a Web page in the Page view.

2. Click the Spelling button (the one with the ABC on it) on the Standard toolbar. This action opens the Spelling dialog box, as shown in Figure 9-1.

Figure 9-1: Check for spelling errors just as you do in Microsoft Word.

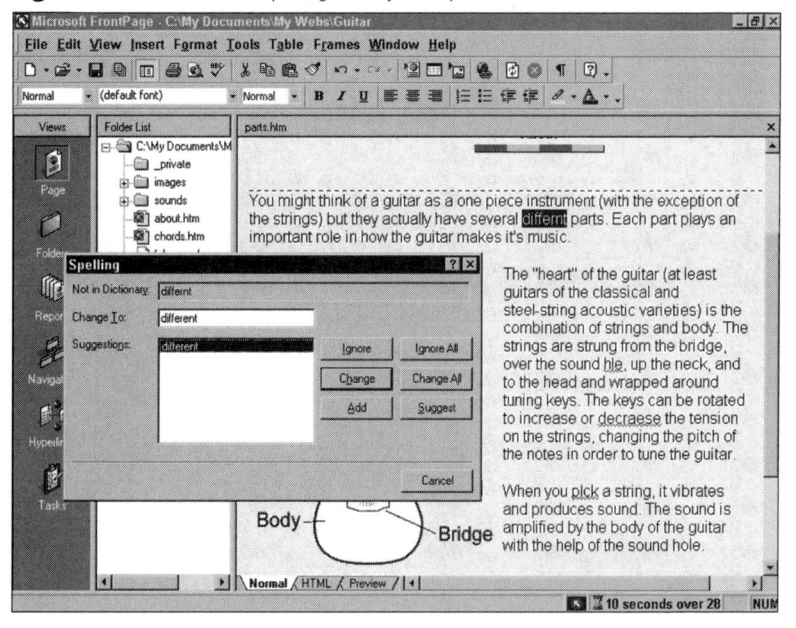

3. FrontPage cycles through all the potential spelling errors on that Web page. You can choose Ignore if you're sure that a particular word is spelled correctly. Select a word in the list of alternative words that FrontPage provides and then choose Change if you want to fix the problem. If you want to add the word to your spelling dictionary,

choose Add. When FrontPage completes its spell-check, it displays a dialog box telling you that the spell-check is complete. Click OK to close the dialog box.

Spell checking your site

FrontPage makes it easy to check all the Web pages in your Web site at one time. This is a welcome convenience, when you think about it. If you have a site with more than a handful of pages, being able to spell-check your entire site at once instead of opening each page separately is a real timesaver. Follow these steps to spell-check your Web site:

 1. Switch to the Folders view and choose Tools➪Spelling. Doing so opens a different Spelling dialog box, as shown in Figure 9-2.

 2. Make sure that the Entire Web box is checked and click Start. FrontPage will go through each Web page and tell you how many words are misspelled in each one.

Figure 9-2:   Spell-checking your entire Web site is a great utility.

 3. Double-click a Web page in the listing to start correcting the errors. FrontPage will open each page in the Page view, one at a time, and show you each spelling error so that you can fix it. When the first Web page is complete, FrontPage asks whether you want to continue to the next document. Choose Next Document if you want to continue checking for errors. Keep going until all your errors are corrected.

4. When you are finished, FrontPage shows you the Spelling dialog box again. Choose Done to close it.

Using the Site Summary report

The Site Summary report should be your best friend when you are maintaining your Web site. It conveniently shows important maintenance-related information about your Web site. Follow these steps to open the Site Summary report:

1. Open your Web and switch to the Reports view.

2. If the Site Summary report is not visible, select Site Summary from the Reporting toolbar. FrontPage displays a list of important information on separate lines, as shown in Figure 9-3.

You can see from Figure 9-3 that there is a lot of information to digest. Each column of the Site Summary report has a unique function:

- **Name:** The column shows the name of a "vital statistic."
- **Count:** This column lists how many files this affects in your Web site.
- **Size:** For statistics that measure how large your files are, this is the total size in kilobytes.
- **Description:** This column describes the vital statistic.

Double-click a line to open a more detailed view of the report. For example, if you double-click Slow pages, FrontPage lists all the pages that meet the criteria and thus qualify as "slow." If you want to know the total size of your Web, just look at the top line of the Site Summary report.

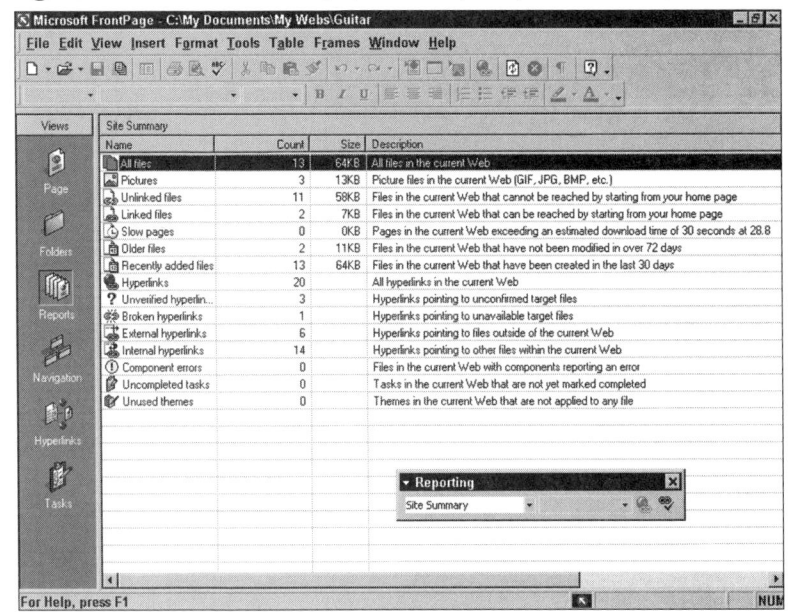

Figure 9-3: The Site Summary report notifies you of possible and real problems.

Working with hyperlinks

Hyperlinks are probably the most troublesome area when it comes to maintaining your Web site. Aside from checking to see that all your internal links work correctly, you need to verify the external Web addresses of any links you have created that load other people's Web pages. If people never changed their Web address or site structure, this wouldn't be as much of a problem as it is. Unfortunately, people (and companies) often change where Web pages are located in their sites.

FrontPage makes checking your links easy. In fact, it does most of the work for you behind the scenes. Follow these steps to verify your hyperlinks and to fix any broken ones:

1. Open your Web site and switch to the Reports view.

2. Double-click on the Unverified or Broken hyperlinks reports. Doing so opens the Broken Hyperlinks report, as shown in Figure 9-4. Links that are fine have an OK next to them, whereas broken links have a small, broken chain-link beside them. Unverified links (links that FrontPage hasn't checked yet) have a question mark next to them.

Figure 9-4: You can see all the verified, broken, and unverified links in this report.

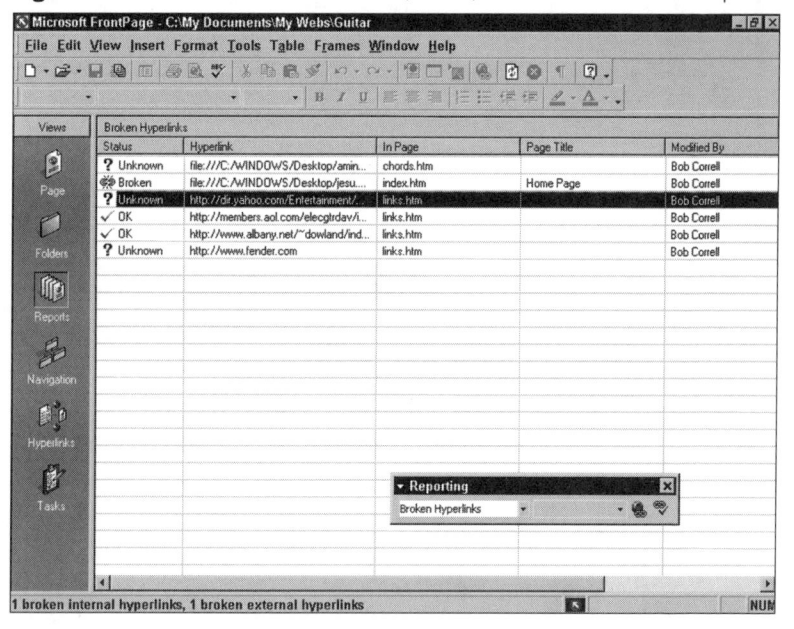

Status	Hyperlink	In Page	Page Title	Modified By
? Unknown	file:///C:/WINDOWS/Desktop/amin...	chords.htm		Bob Correll
Broken	file:///C:/WINDOWS/Desktop/jesu...	index.htm	Home Page	Bob Correll
? Unknown	http://dir.yahoo.com/Entertainment/...	links.htm		Bob Correll
✓ OK	http://members.aol.com/elecgtrdav/i...	links.htm		Bob Correll
✓ OK	http://www.albany.net/~dowland/ind...	links.htm		Bob Correll
? Unknown	http://www.fender.com	links.htm		Bob Correll

1 broken internal hyperlinks, 1 broken external hyperlinks

3. You need to verify unknown hyperlinks. Right-click a hyperlink with a question mark beside it and select Verify. If you are online, FrontPage will go out on the Internet and check whether the Web page you link to is there. If it is, FrontPage updates the graphic to show that the link is okay. If FrontPage cannot verify the link, it labels the link as broken.

4. You need to fix broken hyperlinks. Double-click any hyperlink with a broken chain-link beside it. Doing so opens the Edit Hyperlinks dialog box, as shown in Figure 9-5.

5. Enter a new link address and select Replace to change the link.

Figure 9-5: Enter a new link in the Replace hyperlink with: field to fix broken links.

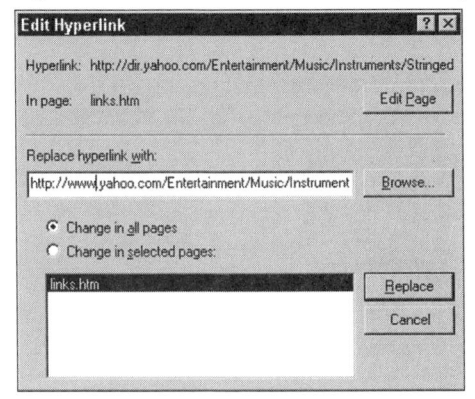

Viewing files that aren't linked

As you continue to update your site, you may find that you "lose" Web pages or graphics. This normally happens when you make changes to a Web page, such as using different graphics, and forget to delete the old graphics from the Web. It can also happen if you replace Web pages with new ones with different names, take the old pages out of your site's navigation structure, but again, forget to delete the files from the Web folder. If the unlinked files are supposed to be a part of your site but you accidentally left them out of your site's structure, you should add them back in through the Navigation view. Either way, you should periodically check for lost files. Follow these steps to view the Unlinked files report:

1. Open your Web and switch to the Reports view.
2. If the Site Summary report is not visible, select it from the Reporting toolbar.
3. Look for the Unlinked files line item in the Site Summary report. This item tells you how many files you have in your Web site that don't have links to them.
4. Double-click the line to open a more detailed report, as shown in Figure 9-6.

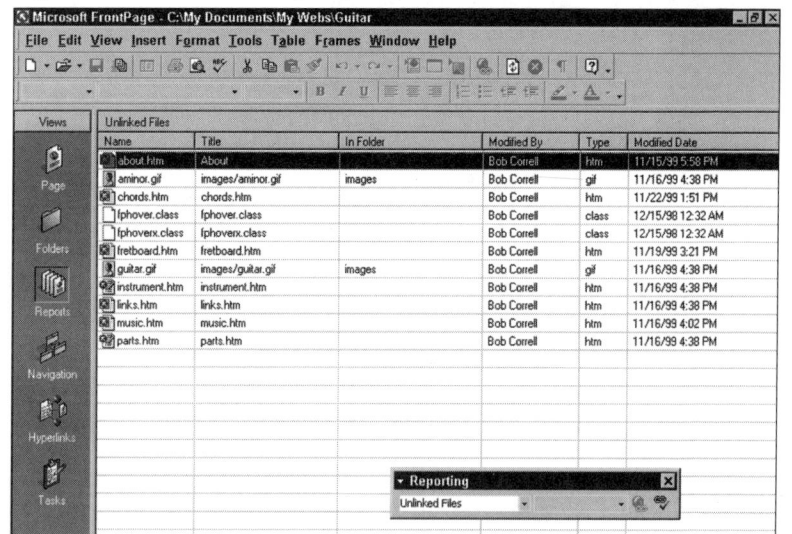

Figure 9-6:   You should regularly check for unlinked files.

Name	Title	In Folder	Modified By	Type	Modified Date
about.htm	About		Bob Correll	htm	11/15/99 5:58 PM
aminor.gif	images/aminor.gif	images	Bob Correll	gif	11/16/99 4:38 PM
chords.htm	chords.htm		Bob Correll	htm	11/22/99 1:51 PM
fphover.class	fphover.class		Bob Correll	class	12/15/98 12:32 AM
fphoverx.class	fphoverx.class		Bob Correll	class	12/15/98 12:32 AM
fretboard.htm	fretboard.htm		Bob Correll	htm	11/19/99 3:21 PM
guitar.gif	images/guitar.gif	images	Bob Correll	gif	11/16/99 4:38 PM
instrument.htm	instrument.htm		Bob Correll	htm	11/16/99 4:38 PM
links.htm	links.htm		Bob Correll	htm	11/16/99 4:38 PM
music.htm	music.htm		Bob Correll	htm	11/16/99 4:02 PM
parts.htm	parts.htm		Bob Correll	htm	11/16/99 4:38 PM

After you know which files aren't linked, you can delete them or add them back into your Web site.

> **Tip:** You should delete any unnecessary files in your Web. When you publish or update your Web site, FrontPage saves all the pages of your Web — linked or unlinked — to your Web server. Having several unlinked files, especially pictures or multimedia files, can significantly lengthen the time it takes you to publish your site.

Updating Your Web Site

One last thought before I let you go. It's very important that you continue to work on your Web site and update it. Always be on the lookout for more information, better pictures, or additional ideas. People will stop visiting your Web site if they think you've gone to sleep on them and have abandoned your own Web site. Here are a few ideas for keeping your Web site current — or at least periodically updating it:

- Add new content as you have the time.
- Write down a schedule for performing maintenance chores — once a week should do it.
- Change your pictures — better, newer, or just different.
- Change your Web site's theme to give it a makeover.
- Experiment with new effects that make your Web more interesting.
- Schedule periodic updates every month and major overhauls every six months.
- Encourage people to give you feedback through e-mail, and then respond by making your Web site meet their needs.

CLIFFSNOTES REVIEW

Use this CliffsNotes Review to practice what you've learned in this book and to build your confidence in doing the job right the first time. After you work through the review questions, the problem-solving exercises, the visual test, and the fun and useful practice projects, you're well on your way to achieving your goal of creating your first Web site with FrontPage 2000.

Q&A

1. FrontPage works with
    a. Web pages
    b. Web sites
    c. Word documents
    d. QRTY files

2. Hyperlinks are
    a. Fast connections
    b. A formatting option
    c. A way of connecting Web pages

3. The Views buttons along the left side on the FrontPage Main window allow you to
    a. Preview your Web pages
    b. See your Web site from different perspectives
    c. See someone else's Web site

4. Where can you get pictures to use in your Web site?
    a. Off the Internet
    b. Scanning them in with your scanner
    c. Using clip art

5. Why do you need a modem to publish your Web site? _____
_____
_____

6. A Web server

   a. Stores your Web site so that people can see it online
   b. Isn't important, so you don't need one
   c. Transfers your Web site from your computer to your ISP

Answers: (1) a and b. (2) c. (3) b. (4) a, b, and c, although you should be careful not to violate any copyrights. You should always check the terms and conditions for use of any graphic, even if it's clip art. (5) You have to connect to the Internet to save your Web site on a Web server. (6) a.

Scenarios

1. You've published your Web site to your Web server and try to view it in your Web browser but it doesn't seem to be there. You should _____
_____
_____

2. Your boss tells you that you need to create a small Web site to get your company online. You've got FrontPage 2000 and a dial-up Internet connection through your office. You should ____
_____
_____

Answers: (1) First, check to see that you are entering the correct Web address in your Web browser. If that isn't the problem, double-check the settings in the Publish Web dialog box to make sure that you stored it in the right location on the Web server and try publishing your Web site again. If that fails, contact your ISP to see whether it can help resolve the problem. Depending on the compatibility options you chose when you created your Web site,

CliffsNotes Review

your Web may require FrontPage Server Extensions be installed on the Web server. (2) Schedule a meeting to start planning your Web site. Decide what your company needs online right away and draw the site on paper. After you have planned it, create it in FrontPage and publish it on your Web server.

Visual Test

Take a look at the FrontPage main screen. Identify the Views icons on the left side and describe what you can do with each one.

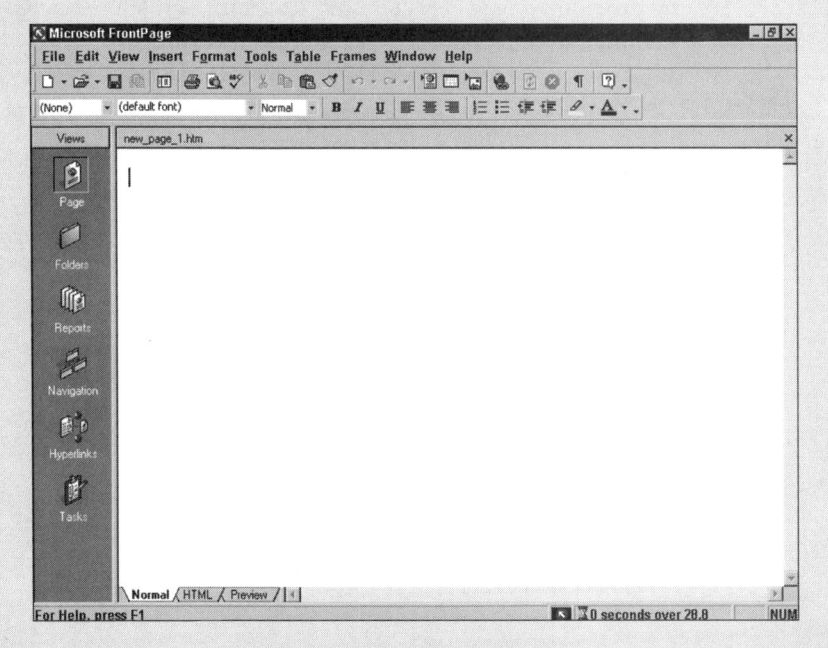

Answers: From top to bottom, the icons are as follows. (1) Page view: Edit your Web pages. (2) Folders view: Track the files and folders of your Web site. (3) Reports view: Run reports that give you detailed information about your site. (4) Navigation view: See how your site is organized. (5) Hyperlinks view: Look at the links to and from each Web page. (6) Tasks view: Create a "to-do" list of tasks necessary to complete your Web site.

Consider This

- Did you know that you can switch themes after you have chosen one and applied it? Open your Web site in FrontPage. If you don't already have a theme, choose the Format➪Theme menu and select one. After you have applied it, preview your site in FrontPage or in your Web browser. Then go back and change themes to another one and compare them.

- Did you know that you can modify themes to suit your taste? Open the Themes dialog box by selecting Format➪Themes and then choose the Modify button. Experiment with choosing different colors, pictures, and text until you have something that looks good; then save your new theme.

Practice Project

1. Create a One Page Web site with FrontPage about your favorite hobby. Visit similar Web sites on the Internet to see what kinds of information they include and how they present it. See Chapter 2 for more information.

2. Visit your ISP's Web site and find its Web site hosting terms and conditions. Look for its phone number and call it if you have any questions. Visit the Microsoft Web site that allows you to find Web Presence Providers and compare their features and terms to your own ISP. Shop around for the best deal. See Chapter 8 for more information.

CLIFFSNOTES RESOURCE CENTER

The learning doesn't need to stop here. CliffsNotes Resource Center shows you the best of the best: links to the best information in print and online about Microsoft FrontPage 2000. And don't think that this is all we've prepared for you; we've put all kinds of pertinent information at www.cliffsnotes.com. Look for all the terrific resources at your favorite bookstore or local library and on the Internet. When you're online, make your first stop www.cliffsnotes.com, where you'll find more incredibly useful information about FrontPage 2000.

Books

This CliffsNotes book is one of many great books about FrontPage 2000 published by IDG Books Worldwide, Inc. So if you want some great next-step books, check out these other publications:

FrontPage 2000 For Dummies Quick Reference, by Damon Dean, is a useful book for both beginners and more experienced users. This handy reference shows you how to integrate FrontPage with Office 2000, collaborate with other people using FrontPage, and use other applications to support FrontPage 2000. (IDG Books Worldwide, Inc.) $12.99.

Teach Yourself Microsoft FrontPage 2000, by David and Rhonda Crowder, features a task-based approach to learning FrontPage 2000 with Personal Workbooks at the end of each chapter. Well-illustrated and extensively cross-referenced, this book is for those who learn by doing. (IDG Books Worldwide, Inc.) $19.99.

FrontPage 2000 For Dummies, by Asha Dornfest, begins by showing you the basics of FrontPage 2000 and then covers more advanced information on themes and active elements, as well as maintaining and publishing your Web. (IDG Books Worldwide, Inc.) $24.99.

FrontPage 2000 Bible, by David Elderbrock and David Karlins, is the book for you if you want to explore every nook and cranny that FrontPage 2000 has to offer. You'll be able to use FrontPage to its fullest potential after reading this comprehensive book. (IDG Books Worldwide, Inc.) $39.99.

It's easy to find books published by IDG Books Worldwide, Inc. You'll find them in your favorite bookstores (on the Internet and at a store near you). We also have three Web sites that you can use to read about all the books we publish:

- www.cliffsnotes.com
- www.dummies.com
- www.idgbooks.com

Internet

Check out these Web sites for more information about FrontPage 2000 and more:

Microsoft FrontPage 2000, www.microsoft.com/frontpage. Serving as Microsoft's official Web site for FrontPage 2000 news, information, support, and downloads, this site contains a wealth of helpful information, especially in the support area.

FrontPage World, www.frontpageworld.com. Here you'll find a site completely devoted to helping you become better at using FrontPage. Numerous tutorials are available online that cover many aspects of FrontPage. You can even sign up for a free newsletter.

OutFront.net, www.outfront.net. You can join a discussion group and newsletter for free at this Web site, and you'll find quite a bit of material for all levels of users.

Microsoft FrontPage Bulletin, www.microsoft.com/frontpage/ bulletins/bulletin.htm. This free, monthly newsletter offers plenty of news and tips for you to read. Visit the site to sign up.

Microsoft FrontPage Newsgroup, news://microsoft.public.frontpage.client. This large newsgroup has many postings from people with all sorts of questions and answers. If you are having trouble with FrontPage, the answer to you question just might be here.

Next time you're on the Internet, don't forget to drop by www.cliffsnotes.com. We created an online Resource Center that you can use today, tomorrow, and beyond.

Magazines & Other Media

Although no print magazines are devoted exclusively to FrontPage 2000, the major computer magazines often feature articles about FrontPage and other helpful FrontPage or Office 2000 tips. You'll have better luck going to an individual magazine's Web site and searching for FrontPage 2000-related features.

PC Magazine is a very well-known and -respected weekly publication that covers the entire PC world from hardware to all sorts of software. (www.zdnet.com/pcmag/)

Windows Magazine is another very useful publication that focuses on Windows and Windows-related software, including FrontPage 2000. www.winmag.com/

You can find these magazines at most bookstores, office supply stores, and even discount stores. To visit these Web sites, simply connect to the Internet, fire up your Web browser, and enter the Web address.

Send Us Your Favorite Tips

In your quest for learning, have you ever experienced that sublime moment when you figure out a trick that saves time or trouble? Perhaps you realized you were taking ten steps to accomplish something that could have taken two. Or you found a little-known workaround that gets great results. If you've discovered a useful tip that helped you use FrontPage 2000 more effectively and you'd like to share it, the CliffsNotes staff would love to hear from you. Go to our Web site at www.cliffsnotes.com and click the Talk to Us button. If we select your tip, we may publish it as part of CliffsNotes Daily, our exciting, free e-mail newsletter. To find out more or to subscribe to a newsletter, go to www.cliffsnotes.com on the Web.

INDEX

A

Active Graphics, 45, 60
Add Rows or Columns dialog box, 75
Add/Remove Programs Properties dialog box, 7
Angelfire, 23
audience, 20, 21

B

backgrounds
  color, 45
  pictures, 45
  sound, 78, 80, 82
banners, 48, 49
bold text, 35, 36
borders
  shared, 46, 47, 48, 49, 52, 53
  table borders, 69, 75, 76
Broken Hyperlinks report, 104
browsers. See Web browsers
bullets
  animated, 45, 60
  bulleted lists, 59, 60
buttons
  animated, 45, 60
  hover, 78, 86, 87
  navigation, 46, 47, 50, 51

C

Cascading Style Sheets (CSS), 20, 45
child pages, 51
clip art, 61, 62, 63
comments, 48, 50, 52, 53
Confirm Delete dialog box, 29
Corporate Presence Wizard, 24
Create E-mail Hyperlink dialog box, 58
Create Hyperlinks dialog box, 56
CSS (Cascading Style Sheets), 20, 45
Customer Support Web template, 23

D

deleting. *See also* Undo feature
  pictures, 37
  text, 37
  Webs, 29
Discussion Web Wizard, 24
domain names, 96
Dynamic HTML (DHTML), 20, 78, 79, 85, 86

E

e-mail links, 57, 58
effects (responses to events), 85
Empty Web template, 23
events, 85

F

File⇨Close Web, 26
File⇨New⇨Web, 24
File⇨Open Web, 27
File⇨Preview in Browser, 38
File⇨Properties, 81
File⇨Publish Web, 96
File⇨Recent Webs, 27
files
  copying, 11
  deleting, 11
  naming, 41
  renaming, 11
  unlinked, 105, 106, 107
floating toolbars, 12
Folder list, 10
folders
  creating, 11
  default document folder, 25
  default graphics folder, 65
  viewing, 11
Folders view, 11
font, 34, 35
Format⇨Dynamic HTML Effects, 85
Format⇨Theme, 44
Formatting toolbar, 32, 33
FrontPage Server Extensions, 94

G

GeoCities, 23
goals, 19, 20
graphics. *See also* themes
 aligning, 62
 animated, 45, 60
 backgrounds, 45
 clip art, 61, 62, 63
 copyright issues, 63
 default folder, 65
 deleting, 37
 file size issues, 61
 pictures, 63, 64, 65
 resizing, 62, 63
 sources, 63
 text wrapping, 62

H

help options
 described, 15, 16
 installing, 6
Help⇨Microsoft FrontPage Help, 15
Help⇨Office on the Web, 16
home pages, 13, 27, 28
.htm extension, 11, 41
hyperlinks. *See* links
Hyperlinks view, 14
HyperText Markup Language (HTML)
 Dynamic HTML (DHTML), 20, 78, 79, 85, 86
 viewing code, 11

I

Import Web Wizard, 24
indenting text, 33, 34
Insert⇨Advanced⇨Plug-In, 83
Insert⇨Component⇨Hover Button, 86
Insert⇨Component⇨Marquee, 87
Insert⇨Horizontal Line, 88
Insert⇨Picture⇨Clip Art, 61
Insert⇨Picture⇨From File, 64
Insert⇨Picture⇨Video, 84
insertion point, 7
installing FrontPage, 6, 7
Internet Service Providers (ISPs), 22, 92, 93
italics, 35, 36

L

lines, horizontal, 78, 88, 89
links
 display, 57
 e-mail, 57, 58
 to external sites, 55, 56, 57
 testing, 103, 104, 105
 viewing, 14, 15
lists
 bulleted, 59, 60
 nested, 60
 numbered, 60

M

main screen, 8, 9, 10, 11, 12, 13, 14, 15
marquees, 78, 87, 88
Menu toolbar, 8
Microsoft Internet Explorer (MSIE), 78
Microsoft Office Update Web site, 16
modems, 91
multimedia. See Dynamic HTML (DHTML); sound; video

N

Navigation Bar Properties dialog box, 50
navigation bars, 46, 47, 48, 49, 50, 51
Navigation view, 13, 42
Netscape Navigator (NNav), 78

O

One Page Web template, 23, 25
Open Web dialog box, 27
opening
 FrontPage, 7, 8
 home pages, 27, 28
 pages, 30, 31
 Webs, 26, 27

P

page banners, 48, 49
Page Options dialog box, 79, 80
Page Properties dialog box, 81
page relationships
 planning, 21
 viewing, 13
Page view, 9, 10, 11

Index

pages
  adding, 41, 42, 43
  child, 51
  creating using templates, 23, 24, 25
  creating using wizards, 24
  introduced, 5
  naming, 41, 49
  parent, 51
  previewing, 37, 38, 39
  slow, 12, 102
  titles, 43, 44
Personal Web template, 23
Picture dialog box, 64
pictures. *See* graphics
planning your site, 18, 19, 20, 21, 22, 23
Plug-In Properties dialog box, 83, 84
Preview in Browser dialog box, 38
previewing pages, 37, 38, 39
Programs⇨Microsoft FrontPage, 7
Project Web template, 23
Publish Web dialog box, 96
publishing your site. *See also* Web hosting
  entire Web, 96, 97
  system requirements, 90, 91
  updates, 97, 98

R

Redo feature, 37
Registered Web Presence Providers, 94
reports
  Broken Hyperlinks, 104
  Site Summary, 12, 102, 103
  Unlinked Files, 106
Reports view, 11, 12

S

Samples (FrontPage component), 6
saving your work, 28
Server Extensions Admin Forms, 6
Server Extensions Resource Kit, 6
shared borders, 46, 47, 48, 49, 52, 53
Shared Borders dialog box, 47
Site Summary report, 12, 102, 103
Slow pages, 12, 102
smart menus, 9
sound
  background, 78, 80, 82
  inline, 78, 83, 84

spell-checking, 100, 101, 102
Spelling dialog box, 100
Standard toolbar, 32
Start⇨Settings⇨Control Panel, 7
starting FrontPage, 7, 8
storyboard, 21, 40
style, 20. *See also* themes
subject matter, choosing, 18, 19
symbols (special characters), 78, 88

T

Table⇨Insert⇨Rows or Columns, 75
Table⇨Properties⇨Table, 69
Table Properties dialog box, 73
Table⇨Properties⇨Table, 69, 73
Table⇨Select⇨Column, 72
Table⇨Select⇨Row, 72
tables
  adding text, 70, 71
  aligning, 74
  aligning content, 71, 72
  borders, 69, 75, 76
  cells, 66, 70
  creating, 67, 68, 69, 70
  deleting columns, 75
  deleting content, 72
  deleting rows, 75
  described, 66, 67
  inserting columns, 74
  inserting rows, 74
  selecting, 72
  selecting elements, 72
  size, 68, 73, 74
templates, 23
testing your site, 92, 93
text
  aligning, 32, 33
  bold, 35, 36
  color, 36
  copying, 32
  cutting, 32
  deleting, 37
  entering, 31
  font selection, 34, 35
  indenting, 33, 34
  italicized, 35, 36
  pasting, 32
  scrolling, 87, 88
  symbols, 78, 88
  underlined, 35, 36
  wrapping around graphics, 62

themes, 6, 44, 45, 46, 111
Title field, 43
Tools⇨Page Options, 79
ToolTips, 16
tutorial installation, 6

U

underlining, 35, 36
Undo feature, 37
uninstalling old versions, 7
Unlinked Files report, 106
updating your site, 97, 98, 107
upgrading to FrontPage 2000, 7

V

video, 84
View⇨Folder list, 10
viewing your site
  folder structure, 11
  HTML code, 11
  hyperlinks, 14, 15
  page relationships, 13
  pages, 9, 10, 11
  site info, 12, 102, 103
Views bar, 9, 10, 11, 12, 13, 14, 15

W

Web address, 95, 96
Web browsers. *See also* Microsoft Internet Explorer (MSIE); Netscape Navigator (NNav)
  designing for older versions, 20, 45, 77
  designing for specific browsers, 78, 79, 80
  introduced, 5
  multimedia capabilities, 78
Web hosting, 22, 23, 93, 94, 95
Web pages. *See* pages
Web servers, 22, 23, 93, 94, 95
Web sites. *See* Webs
Webs
  closing, 26
  creating, 23, 24, 25, 26
  defined, 5
  deleting, 29
  opening, 26, 27
  testing, 92, 93
wizards, 23, 24
World Wide Web, 17

X

Xoom, 23